WILL NEVER GIVE UP!

FOR THE

TEENAGER

By Derek W. Clark

Printed in the United States of America.

FIRST EDITION

I WILL NEVER GIVE UP FOR THE TEENAGER
WRITTEN BY DEREK W.CLARK

WWW.IWILLNEVERGIVEUP.COM

CONTACT DEREK CLARK AT
DEREK@IWILLNEVERGIVEUP.COM

Edited by Michael Laemmle
Email: mrlaemmle@gmail.com

Cover design by Adreana Shavers
WWW.BOLDGRAPHIXINC.COM

PUBLISHED BY NEVER LIMIT YOUR LIFE
OFFERING LIFE COACHING AND SEMINARS
To Book Workshops and Seminars call 1-800-980-0751

WWW.NEVERLIMITYOURLIFE.COM

ISBN 13: **978-0-9825134-0-8**

PREFACE

WHASSUP!!! I am so excited about having the chance to share my story with you. A story about never giving up and overcoming adversity. I know that after reading my book, you will be able to walk away with a renewed vision on how to triumph as a teenager. I want to share with you some of the experiences I went through as a young man. I want to share with you how I overcame hopelessness and turned my disadvantage into an amazing advantage. More than anything, I want you to know that you too can overcome any obstacle that is set before you. You are resilient, strong and courageous! You are made to never give up, to conquer your fears, to turn your weaknesses into strengths, and to be transformed by greatness.

Life is chaotic, full of unexpected twists and turns. You cannot and will not always have control over the events in your life. Bad experiences are going to happen, no matter what. But as I hope you will learn through this book, the one thing you most definitely can control is the way you respond to these situations. You control your own attitude. You decide what meaning these events will have in your life. You decide how they will affect you.

Get ready! You are about to be transformed into a confident, determined young person, endowed with the unwavering perseverance to achieve your unlimited potential. This is *your* life - NEVER GIVE UP!

Derek

By the way, Check out my newest rap I wrote called "This Is My Life". It's as real as it gets...yunno...without the cuss words....haha...C-ya—-Derek
You can hear it at <u>www.IWillNeverGiveUp.com</u>

THIS IS MY LIFE

Verse 1

Everyday is a struggle, if I could change my past, I'd be staying out of trouble and I know it would last, but this is my life, a battle for my fate, save my soul before it gets too late, Who's gonna win and who's gonna lose, I never thought I'd be wearing these shoes, of life, man it don't feel right, when am I gonna see the light and feel the light,Walk with me, someone walk with me, come on dad yeah just talk to me, Have you ever thought about me in your life, why'd you wanna kill me and take away my life, I'm your blood dad, I'm your son dad, yeah its messed up knowing that I never knew my dad, who, didn't want to be a dad, wassup with that, don't understand, but I gotta get past. Hey daddy daddy where you been, in the jail cell one again. You ain't never seen me smile, never seen me walk, never seen me talk, never never seen me rock, this microphone, yeah this is my home, let me let me out of my pain, cuz I know I'm not alone. Yeah these are my peeps and I'm telling how I feel, this is no secret and I'm keeping it real, now mama, why'd you have to run away, why'd you leave me alone, why'd you have to make me pay, for my daddy's sins, daddy's eyes and daddy's pain and daddy's lies, now I'm on the outside yeah looking inside, I'm a bust this curse even if I gotta die.

*Chorus
This is my life, this is my story, this is my pain, this is my glory

Verse 2

Everyone loses something sometime, I never thought I'd have to lose my mind, yeah lose my world, lose my soul and lose the one's who gave me hope, now my sisters been killed and my brothers been killed and my friends been killed, when am I gonna heal?

In the snap of a finger and my life gets jacked, in
the snap of a finger now my life feels trapped,
where the love was, yeah hate begins, now I'm
mad at the world cuz the pain won't end, I'll
cover up the hurt, I'll cover up the shame, I'm
caught in the middle of a hurricane of pain, so
pain pain, show me what you got, now I'm never
gonna let anyone back in my heart, til my wrists
start to bleed and I don't feel the need of living
this life, will someone hold me, man I need you,
say a prayer for me, yeah let me believe that you
believe in me.

*Chorus
This is my life, this is my story, this is my pain,
this is my glory

Verse 3

I'm in the middle of darkness, I need light, I'm
tired of the pain and it's stealing from life, Do I
play a role? Do I play a victor? Do I play a victim? Or do I blame the system? A moment of
truth D and this is it, tell me now man, are you
really gonna make it, my life's been like a shattered mirror, putting all the pieces back together,
but its still not clear, If I can't see me, I'm gonna
quit, cuz no one's ever told me I could really

ever make it, but here I am, in the ditch, I'm getting buried, dirt on my head, man its getting scary, I gotta get up, I gotta get up, I gotta get up, someone's yelling Never Give Up! This is my life man, I gotta be strong, I'm starting to rise up now and then I fall, take a chance D and try again, reach, reach, reach,-try again,
With the power of God and the faith of a man, If I believe, I Believe I Can, Rise up and never give up, come on man-I got the spirit, now get up, on my knees, slowly on my feet, here I come now yeah shaking off defeat, now I'm up and I don't want to ever ever die, I got the power now back in my life, no one's ever ever gonna hold me down, with my hopes, my dreams, my soul holding that crown, of glory, yeah this is my story, so here I am, man tell me your story.

*Chorus
This is my life, this is my story, this is my pain, this is my glory

CONTENTS

MY DEDICATION

To my biological mother - thank you for giving me the precious gift of life. Despite all of life's hardships and challenges, it is also filled with joy and laughter and awe-inspiring beauty. To be alive, to be here on Earth, is the greatest gift in the universe. And thank you too, for giving me away so that I could have a better life than the one you were able to provide. I didn't always understand your reasons for doing what you did, but your true sacrifice has made me a passionate, empathetic, persevering, loving and determined person. Because of my suffering, I am a stronger man!

I thank you for leaving me alone all those years so that I could find myself. Your absence allowed me to grow, without holding on to the empty hope that you might come back for me. So many foster children get messed up because their mothers and fathers keep coming around and randomly sticking their noses into their child's life. This does nothing more than give the child false hopes that his or her parents are going to one day bring them back into the family. When this doesn't happen, the disappointment is devastating. Life becomes confusing and hopeless. The child, believing he is responsible for his rejection, is consumed with self-doubt and guilt. I am truly thankful that you did not torment me in this way.

Although we don't talk, there is so much I'd like to tell you. I want to let you know that life was tough for me. So much of the time I was lonely and afraid. It was not easy feeling like a lamb among wolves. I had to learn how to survive, and to deal with what life handed me. It chokes me up when I stop and think about the frightened little boy that I used to be—but it keeps me real. I wish I could go back in time and reassure him. I wish I could\ tell him everything is going to turn out all right, that this period of sorrow and pain will not last.

To my foster mother and father - I consider you my Mom and Dad. In the end, I credit you both with all my successes. Thank you for your undying patience throughout the years. There are so many reasons to be grateful to you. I thank you for leaving the TV off, and for not having video games to play with, even when all my friends did. Your strictness on this point meant that I could nurture my talents and abilities, and turn into the hardworking and loving person you raised. Because of your discipline, laziness is not in my bones. I thank you for introducing me to animals, sports and Boy Scouts – but I especially thank you for introducing me to music. Thanks for music camp too, and for cheering me on at those competitions and events. Thank you for all the great times, and for the memories, both happy and sad.

To my beautiful, angelic, and loving wife! You are amazing! Thanks for being my biggest cheerleader, and for your incredible ability to be a great spouse and an unbelievable mother. Your laughter and love inspires me. I love your gentleness, reassurance, open mind, unconditional love, and acceptance of me for who I am. I am so grateful that we met and have been able to share our lives! I can't even begin to image who I'd be without you.

To my four beautiful children - Remington, Ozmond, Trayton and Montgomery. I never suspected that children could bring such deep and lasting joy into a person's life. Your bright smiles can make the strongest man weak. The loving hugs and happy screams of "Daddy's home!" make me melt. You are all amazing. You have brought me so many happy tears, so many smiles and bursts of laughter. I never thought my love could be so strong. You are my flesh and blood, and my heroes, because you saved me from a poisonous past. I learn from each one of you every day. You are living proof that life makes me better as I go along.

To all the Foster Children and every Teenager suffering in this world: TAKE A DEEP BREATH! This suffering is only one small part of your big, adventurous life! Don't let pain consume your entire existence, and don't use it as an excuse for your down-falls. I know you may feel lost because nobody really wants to call you their own, but listen—you have the power to take decisive actions and break the cycle of self-doubt! One day you will have the power to do right by creating a family of your own. That's what life is really about! Imagine creating the kind of family you wish you'd been a part of! You will make it if you surround yourself with good friends who make good choices and set good examples for you. Remember to seek out positive people and positive situations. The wrong environment can lead you down a destructive, purposeless, and unrewarding path.

Remember, your circumstances are not your fault. For many years I thought I was to blame for my parents giving me up. It was late in life when I realized it wasn't my fault. I WAS ONLY FIVE YEARS OLD! I was the kid and they were the adults. Don't let your emotions poison you. Don't be a nothing! Be everything you want to be, and keep on dreaming. Never let anybody tell you that you can't do something, or be somebody. Don't ever let anyone take your dreams away from you. Don't ever be a slave to drugs or alcohol; otherwise you are just another casualty. Use your tough experiences, get nourishment from them; they will make you mentally stronger than the average kid. Believe in yourself! Bulletproof your soul! The future is unwritten; strive to create the future you desire.

At times, loneliness is a virtue. It allows you to discover yourself. Don't ever, *ever*, hold yourself back from crying. Crying cleanses and refreshes the soul. By the same token, don't forget to laugh. When I was going through rough times, the best medicine was a good, deep belly-laugh. Just as important, don't be afraid to laugh at yourself. I've always liked being the clown. Laughing at ourselves helps put things in perspective, lightens the load, and can make our problems seem less daunting and more easily manageable.

Don't hate! Hatred is the real poison of the soul. You must learn to forgive. Secretly, I nurtured a lot of poisonous feelings throughout my life. I sometimes tortured my own soul and liked it. I enjoyed dwelling on and nurturing feelings of hatred. But if hate and anger do overcome you, you can use the power of these emotions for positive ends. Channel their enormous energy into something productive; a painting, a song, school project or workout. Intense feelings were like a fire that drove my desire to prove to the world that I wasn't "a nobody." Emotions of any kind, if properly directly, can be a stimulus to great things.

If there is one thing I have learned, it is this: If I Can Fly, You Can Fly! Let your spirit fly so that you may one day help another person to fly! Never Give Up!!!

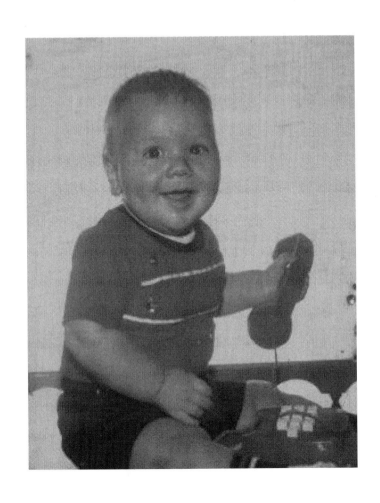

MY LIFE TODAY DOESN'T HAVE TO BE CONTROLLED BY MY PAST

This is the true story of my life. A life in which abuse, loneliness, and dark nights of despair rattled the very bones of my body, drained the tears of my spirit, shattered my mind into a million fragments, and for awhile left me plodding through life as an empty shell, a lost and helpless soul. I have breathed the air of the unloved, and suffered deep psychological and spiritual wounds due to abandonment at an early age by my mother and father. I have blamed myself for a past over which I had no control. My trust in people was displaced with hostility and anger. And yet, ***my spirit would not be broken.*** I have fought for survival in the name of love, powered by a dogged will whose voice never stopped telling me to NEVER GIVE UP!

I was a five year-old kid, and already a survivor of appalling events. I have never known my father. My mother, having given up on me, placed me in the County Social Services Foster Care System. She was desperate to be rid of me. The saddest, most inexplicable part of this was that she kept my younger brother and older sister. I was devastated knowing I had been deleted from my family. I was now motherless and fatherless. I loved my mother, brother and sister, but my love for them wasn't enough for her to keep me in the family.

My mother claimed she could not control me, and that I was a "devil." But I now know she was the one out of control. I was the child and she was the adult. I am not to blame for the predicament I found myself in. But that is life; it is unfair.

There are millions of kids who have been given up on, and I hold their parents completely responsible. The ignoble actions of parents will always be remembered by their children. I know, because that five year-old foster child still lives within me, constantly striving to be empowered, to make his insecurities my own. But I refuse to be a victim; I am a conqueror.

There is no question; the mental and physical struggles of my life have proved very difficult to overcome. They say the first five years of a child's life are the most critical to his or her development, and that children soak up everything they experience like a sponge. I agree. I have seen my own children sponge both my strengths and weaknesses. Kids watch their parents, and mimic what they observe. The influence of my first five years contributed to many destructive behaviors throughout my life. I often wished I had been given away at birth, so that I wouldn't have had to endure the memories and nightmares which have haunted me these many years.

There is always a lesson to be learned from adversity. I have learned many such lessons the hard way, but have found there is a light at the end of the tunnel. The light that leads us out of the darkness is the positive energy that comes to surround those who continually search for what life has to offer. The answer is always within. By harnessing this positive energy you can accomplish anything. Nothing has ever held me back from "going for it." I have not let anyone or anything stop me from making my dreams a reality. I keep on keeping on. I am an unstoppable force. I am headstrong and know exactly what I want. I have always trusted my intuition.

My search for life's meaning eventually brought me through a baptism by fire, which cleansed my soul. I am like the mystical "Phoenix" that has risen from its own ashes, a resurrected soul, a lost boy who evolved into a man. In life's journey, I was meant to shine. It is this journey in which fractured souls are made whole again. It is this journey in which wounds are healed and pain is finally replaced by love and peace.

This is a bitter-sweet story filled with real blood, real tears, unthinkable pain, turmoil, hope, love, success; and finally, significance. This is the true story of a fearless boy who fought for his life and won.

This book is for anyone who is suffering emotionally, mentally, and physically in their life. I am not a doctor, nor do I hold a degree in psychology. I can't claim to have graduated from a prestigious university with a 4.0 G.P.A. I am not here to "fix" you or put your life together in the way I see fit. I am here to help you first identify, and then to *modify* your thought processes. Unhappy thoughts lead to unhappy actions, with the end result being an unhappy life. We all want a happy life and peaceful state of mind. I believe that what you think you are or can be, you have the power to be. The challenge is to become the person you want to be.

A person doesn't need a college degree to deeply touch another's soul. We are all human and feel emotions, whether it is fear, love, happiness, anger or sadness. People can make an impact on others in dramatic, life-changing ways, both negative and positive.

My credentials are relevant, credible and simple. They are "real life" disasters and triumphant experiences. I am in touch with my inner self and thought that now, having overcome, I would take the opportunity to share my experiences; those experiences which I have survived, and how I have thrived in spite of them. We are all imperfect and sometimes choose to unwisely focus on our suffering. We become attached to our pain, making it a part of who we are. But there comes a time when we can no longer relinquish our minds and bodies to the victim mentality. We must become mind-conquerors.

Your life has meaning! You are significant! You are who you want to be! Believe that! There is a real price to pay for a true smile, the kind that will shine forth from somewhere deep inside you, but it's a price worth paying!

DON'T LET EXCUSES
CONTROL YOUR LIFE

Today is a brand new day. Every day you wake up is like a fresh white canvas ready to be painted upon. How have you painted the pictures of all your yesterdays? And how are you going to paint all your tomorrows? A good indication is how you paint your todays.

I have found that being grateful for the air I breathe allows me to put my life in perspective. It inspires me to get the most out of every day. As far as I know, I have one life to live. I intend to live it. Time and time again, I have seen people who have died long before they're actually dead and in the grave. They are living miserable lives, but why? Because they hold onto something—some pain, some insecurity, some fear or some hatred—that will not allow them to live their life to the fullest. It's like they are dead, yet living, a zombie.

I believe there is a reason why they are not living life to their fullest potential. There is even a word for it: pity. Or better yet, living a pitiful life, a life full of excuses. These people think, "Oh I can't do that, I am not good enough, I am a loser, it will never work for me, etc...." They adopt this way of thinking, and it literally controls them, warping every aspect of their life. They become *limited* instead of *limitless*.

Say to yourself right now: "I AM LIMITLESS! NOTHING CAN HOLD ME BACK! I HAVE END-LESS POTENTIAL AND ENDLESS ENERGY! I CAN DO ANYTHING I PUT MY MIND TO!"

Don't ever let an excuse steal victory from out of your hands. Attachment to your problems steals far more from your life than you might imagine. Instead of being attached to your problems, why not strive to nurture an attachment to your dreams? A human being only has so much energy, a limited amount. Where we direct our mental and emotional resources directly impacts our lives. Dwelling on problems and making excuses only brings despair, depression and exhaustion. Dreams bring hope and energy. Having dreams to strive for will literally change your entire life. Excuses do nothing but steal from your greatness. Look around you; the world is full of excuses. Here are just a few. Have you used any of these?

"I'm afraid."
"It's too hard."
"I can't because…."
"I wish I could, but…."
"It's too risky."
"I will fail if I try."

"I'm not smart enough."
"Nothing good ever happens to me."
"I tried already."
"I'm not strong enough."
"I'm not tall enough."
"I'm not pretty enough."
"I'm not skinny enough."
"I don't have any money."
"I'm not rich enough."
"I don't have the time."
"I'm not meant to make it."
"I'm not talented enough."
"I'm scared that I will mess it up."
"I'm not good enough."
"I always lose."
"I'm worried what people will think about me."
"It stresses me out."
"It's not going to work."
"I'm cursed."
"Everything I touch just doesn't work out."
"I don't know where to start."
"I just don't know how."
"I will never be able to…."
"I can't do that."
"I am not even going to try."
"I'm too old."
"I don't have a college degree."
"My dad never showed me how."
"My mom never showed me how."
"I can't keep up, I'm too slow."

"It will never work."

"Nothing good ever happens for me."

"I'm not good at anything."

"I've tried it a million times."

"How can I do this? I have never done it before."

"It won't work."

I have found that fear of taking action, fear of throwing caution to the wind and just going for it, is the most destructive of all excuses. It controls your outlook on life. Your perception of life—its possibilities for joy and success—becomes limited and narrow. You come to believe that you can't accomplish anything new. But with a little courage, you can always accomplish something unique and unprecedented. In fact, the more unprecedented your goal, the more courage you will need! If you live an excuse-free life, I know that means you have a free and open future, full of possibilities. You have freed yourself! You are now free to try anything! You are free from the fear of failure. You will never go anywhere in life if you don't try.

Don't take ownership of an excuse. This is to say, don't attach yourself to one. No possible excuse is worth limiting your life. For example, I could easily have said that I'm unable to give love because my parents gave me up, and if they gave me up, I shouldn't be able to love or trust anyone. But why look at it like that? How would I ever really know what love was without lack of love? Now that is a deep thought. How could I ever give love if it had not been taken away from me? I know I have something to give that is beneficial because I've experienced what life is like when it's lived without love. I know love is a very valuable thing and is essential to living a happy and meaningful life. It is better to love and give your heart away then just hold your feelings in and never experience true joy. Love is meant to heal, not hurt, but you have to give love in order to receive it. And to give it, you must have the courage to make yourself a little vulnerable.

Excuses become part of our identities, and soon we become afraid to get out of our comfort zones. People tend to strive to live a life within a certain level of comfort and ease. But guess what? Life can and will be overwhelming at times. I don't know anyone who has lived a long life and said that it was always easy. Life is full of surprises, and not all of them pleasant ones. You must go beyond the boundaries of comfort you have set for yourself.

If you let excuses control your life, expect to never find a true and lasting happiness. Excuses are meant to reign you in and hold you back. They truly rob you of your dreams. They send you on detours and chip away at your self-determination. They take from your spirit and diminish your love of life, until you slowly become boxed in and, eventually, afraid to bust out of the box.

Most of the excuses I hear have to do with FEAR. Did you know that becoming a champion at something starts in the mind, in your own thoughts? A champion's mentality starts with an inner belief that he or she can be better than the best, by being faster, smarter and stronger. They are determined. They believe it, speak it, practice it, and live it. In this life, everyone is born with the potential to be a champion. But somewhere along the way, people allow others to break down their dreams. They allow others to destroy their belief in themselves. These negative people try to replace others God-given gifts, talents and abilities with fear, a sense of defeat, laziness, and feelings of worthlessness. What these negative people don't understand is that the gifts of the soul can never be taken away. They can be wasted, but the soul is resilient and will bounce back. If you are in tune with your own spirit and soul, you will be able to bounce back, and your inner greatness will always overcome your weakness. Your difficulties were not meant to defeat you.

I believe that Fear takes you backwards and Faith moves you forward. Fear is nothing more than a made-up boogey man, here to scare you into believing you can't achieve anything in life. Your faith is the fuel that will focus your energy. The energy will thrust you forward, and soon you will desire to live only in a self-determined way. You will be ready to persevere, knowing that you are never going to give up. You must know inside your soul that you really can achieve your dreams. Live the feeling, this faith, and the feeling will breathe life into your aspirations.

Everyone has a destiny, but you must be ready to work hard to achieve it. The level and intensity of your destiny is determined by the level and intensity of your own desire. Some work hard to build theirs; others destroy their own destiny through laziness. Your destiny will be a direct reflection of your efforts. I don't believe your destiny will simply come to you. You have to exercise will, you have to go out and get it. You have the tools within you to have a purpose and persevere until you reach it.

It is important to remember that you can also save another person's life after you have saved your own. What I mean by this is that you can help another person to see value in their life, but this is best done when you see the value in your own. You can help others believe that they too can give a great gift to this world if only they never give up. Be a positive role model for others, and don't be afraid to say hello to someone in the hall or on the street. You never know how their life is going, or what troubles are weighing on their minds. Just by your small effort to say hello, you may have just saved their life. Maybe they were on their way to end it all – you truly never know.

The best way to live life is with selflessness, not selfishness. By giving to this world and offering your talents to it, you are literally changing the course of this crazy planet. You are helping to create a more enriching and peaceful Earth. Check out the lyrics:

"Well I confess that I could have been everything you said,
but I didn't listen to you, cuz I thought I knew what was best.
No one ever told me anything that I wanted to hear,
So now I suffer cuz I'm stubborn, gotta get out of here.
Then I heard....

(Chorus)
You can be anything if you want to try, fly to the moon or save a life.
You can be anything if you want to try, never give up, this is your life
Hey give it a try, give it a try.

Well I pulled myself out of hell and did something right, can't you tell
That I'm standing here singing my songs, I've done more right than wrong,
My hearts on track, yeah I got my life back,

And you can be anything and that's a fact.

You can be anything if you want to try, fly to the moon or save a life.
You can be anything if you want to try, never give up, this is your life
Hey give it a try, give it a try.

So *Never Give Up*. Find the faith within to fuel your spirit. Believe in your vision. Believe in yourself and believe that you have a lot to offer. Use your life to put your stamp on the world. You are unique. Only you can offer that one thing the world needs. Thomas Edison tried over 10,000 times to invent the light bulb. Through perseverance and hard work, he did. You may not be here to invent the light bulb, but trust me when I tell you that you have your own gift to offer this world. Believe it!

DISCOVER YOUR SELF-DETERMINATION. BELIEVE IN YOURSELF!

You have the strength to make it through the ups and down of your life. This book has a purpose, and it is to help you overcome limiting and negative thoughts. It will inspire the courage take action. You will learn the four letter word you can say over and over again for inner strength. It will show you how I used the POWER of taking ACTION in my life, and how you can take action in yours. It will show you how a mind-conqueror survives and thrives from the battle within. It will encourage you to improve your personal life through clear and lucid thinking. It will help you develop trust in yourself and give you the confidence needed to overcome.

We have all been engaged in a war with ourselves at one time or another. Now is the time for rethinking our strategies and winning the war once and for all. You must grow beyond your limiting thoughts, and have the courage and conviction to tell yourself "I WILL NEVER GIVE UP!"

Determination can change your life forever. There is a four letter word that is woven into the fabric of my soul, and that word is WILL. To have the WILLPOWER to succeed is not an easy task.

Having a purpose encourages self-determination. It all starts with a belief, an idea that can create a powerful destiny.

The seed of purpose is planted deep within you. If you water that seed, energy will be created. Energy creates motion, motion creates action, action creates results, results create achievement, achievement creates self-confidence, and self confidence creates the mindset that you can and WILL achieve anything you desire.

Through determination, we can turn our bad habits into good habits. We can conquer our fears and turn a life of tragedy into a life of triumph. Having determination gives you the strength to conquer all of life's obstacles. I have always found a way to bust through the walls of self-doubt.

I normally ignore negative people who throw off a very toxic vibe. I don't want to surround myself with self-doubters and believers in "doom-and-gloom." I know that some of you can change your life right now, by changing your friends. Hang out with people who are going places in life, people who dare to dream of changing the world and of making it a better place. These are the kind of friends you want. The ones who are willing to dream big, not the ones who belittle your dreams, or tell you that you will never be anything or do anything great. I once heard a saying about hanging out with questionable friends: "Do you want to fly with the eagle or fly with the ducks?" The eagle is the highest-soaring bird. As for myself, I know I want to be flying with them, and going where they go.

One thing you have to realize is that there are going to be times when you will have to let go of your friends. Some friends are good for certain seasons of your life, but if the friendship is destructive to yourself and your goals, don't try to talk someone into staying your friend. There is a reason in your great destiny that someone will walk in your life and then walk out. Friends should not be like eggshells, where you have to walk very carefully around them. Friends don't control and manipulate, they help you become a better person. So don't be afraid to let the wrong friends go, so that the right friends will come into your life.

I've had bad friends and good friends. My good friends helped out along the way and looked out for me. They encouraged me to make good choices. I was one of those guys who nobody expected to do anything great, but it turned out that I did. Because of my past, a lot of people figured I was destined to do nothing better than rot in a jail cell or become a drug addict. But I rose up and decided that I wanted to be somebody. I didn't want to carry on the cycle of my parents. I had a clean slate, so I made a promise to myself that I would do big things. Never would I surrender my dreams or retreat from a challenge. Heck yeah, I made lots of mistakes, and was almost down for the count more than once. But don't ever count Derek Clark out! Each time, I would rise back up from the knockdown, arising stronger and stronger. I now know that my adversities were making me stronger. I started to have that fire burning within, the fire to Never Give Up!

The first step I took toward living a more rewarding life was speaking the right kind of words. I starting speaking words that inspired great intentions, words that brought out the best in me, words that produced encouraging thoughts. Words have power, especially when there is strong faith behind them. Words without faith are like garbage coming out of your mouth. They don't amount to anything. Did you know that the words you speak and think with can be prophetic? They can completely change the quality of your life, for good or bad. When you speak negative words, words of pity and defeat, you are going to attract these negative forces into your life. When you speak positive words of faith and victory, you are going to attract that kind of power.

So ask yourself whether if, when you speak, you are speaking words of faith or words of fear. Then step back and observe what comes your way. I believe the more you talk about something, the more you turn that something into a reality. So if you look in the mirror and say, "I am fat" – and then keep saying that day after day - chances are you are going to stay overweight. But if you tell yourself you are a *skinny fat-burning machine*, I believe you will attract the type of positive energy that will inspire you to shed some pounds. You will take actions that are directly related to the words you're saying to yourself. The words will be positive, and this positivity will energize you into taking proactive steps toward bringing about the reality. So be very careful how you talk to yourself. It takes practice to be aware of what you are saying. Often the words fly out of the mouth so fast that you find yourself reacting to your own thoughts. Be controlled with your mouth as well as your thoughts. It will lead you to a richer and happier life.

There is much to be said about being in control of your thoughts, words and actions. I was a very slow learner when it came to this kind of control. I used to be much more explosive when confronted. No doubt about it, I was very much a reactor to life's circumstances, and for a very long time. It seemed like my reactions were always negative. Study your own typical reactions. Are they positive or negative?

A painful past is a series of stepping stones to a great future. I may have had a very rough start, but once I started focusing on having a great ride and living in the moment, I felt released. I felt like I had wings. I once heard this saying: "The bigger your problem, the greater your destiny can be." Extraordinary people have faced extraordinary difficulties. So get out there and meet the challenges! But remember to choose your words and thoughts carefully. We cannot speak defeat and expect to have success in our life. Imagine overcoming all the negative thoughts and words in your life, and replacing them with only words of wisdom and victory. I strive for that type of control. If I had known this as a teenager, I would have begun excel much earlier than I did.

NEVER LIMIT YOURSELF...FLY

The message of this book is for everyone, though the book itself is intended for teenagers. I desired it be written in a style simple enough that people of almost any age could read it and relate to the story, in the hope that they be inspired to evaluate and, if need be, change their life, no matter how daunting their circumstances. Our choices determine our outcomes. If you make good choices, you will never give up, and choosing to never give up is the first and most important choice you make. The world will often impose its own idea of who you are and who you can be, but don't succumb to those judgments. You are who you decide you will be. You have the power, don't relinquish it. Strength comes from taking action. Adversity makes the strong stronger and the weak weaker.

I consider my actions and thoughts to be those typical of a strong person, but I wasn't always strong. A difficult early life made me the man I am today. This book will take you on a journey through my life. It is a collection of thoughts, case histories, poems, journal entries, lessons I have learned as a father, and song lyrics, many written in my darkest and loneliest hours. These are my reactions to the struggles life has thrown at me.

I won't lie and tell you I was the happiest kid. I struggled mentally and physically. There were traumatic experiences throughout my youth and I had to learn to live with them. I was given up by my own Mom at an early age, yet inexplicably she kept my brother and sister. I was so scared and alone, and these feelings persisted on through my teenage years.

For me, this negative energy wasn't channeled into depression and melancholy. I wasn't a depressed kid who was withdrawn and picked on. I actually went the opposite way, and was filled with aggression and anger.

The fact is, I was a very angry kid with problems trusting, loving, and accepting others. These difficulties are described in the journal entries which I made throughout the first twenty years of my life. Deep down I believe I was a happy kid, whose anger and mistrust arose from the miserable life experiences which I had to endure at such a young age.

As a young man, a fire raged within me. I could no longer trust adults and constantly defied authority, always eager to challenge the wisdom of my elders. I was not fearful, I was fearless, albeit not always in a healthy way. Some deep mistrustful instinct was triggered inside me, and knowing I could no longer trust adults, I felt I had to survive on my own and could only trust myself. While other kids were happy with their families, I was with foster families who often provided me little more than a bed to sleep on and food to eat. I knew these families weren't my real one, and the parents weren't my real Mom and Dad. Adding to the feeling of being lost in limbo, was that I never really knew how long I might be at a particular foster home. This uncertainty kept me constantly on edge.

I was hurt deeply when my mother abandoned me to the foster care system. If I couldn't trust my own mother, how could I trust anyone else? It brings tears to my eyes even now as I write this book, remembering the child I was, unable to trust another living person. I was a five year-old kid who was about to learn the art of mental survival on his own.

It is my hope that through this book, I will both bring healing to myself and inspire others to find the strength within. I want others to develop the power necessary to thrive, to keep despair and loneliness at bay, and not allow destructive habits of mind to take you down a road of perpetual self-torture. It is unfortunate, but it seems we humans like to torture ourselves by blaming ourselves for the circumstances of our life, and those aspects of it that seem beyond our control. But life is out of control. The only thing we can control is our attitude. That is it! Life may be what happens when we're making other plans, but we own our thoughts and control our outlook on life.

We alone are the ones who are capable of not letting life take a bite out of us, or get the best of us. The strength and will to survive each day comes from within, and we can approach life with an attitude of gratitude.

It is a choice to be strong. It's that simple. We choose to stop the self-torture, and it is ourselves who free us from our own mental prisons. We often keep ourselves from doing great things and put up imaginary walls to block us in. But we can just walk out the imaginary door. There is always a door for walking in, just as there is always an exit door for walking out. The mind always seeks an exit strategy. But you have to find it where it is hidden amongst all the mental clutter. Don't ever tell yourself there is no way out of your present situation. Remember, you are in control. Your thoughts are under your control. And when you take control of your thoughts, you can build the life you've always wanted.

It is my deepest hope that this book will inspire you to Never Give Up! Never succumb to the negative thoughts which may be weighing you down. Thoughts are very heavy and can give you a false outlook on life. The "victim mentality" is one of the worst things that can enter a person's mind. It will change you mentally, physically, spiritually, and financially. Not only that, but you could very well pass this destructive mindset on to your children, just like any disease. The sins of the father are visited on the son.

By setting the good example of personal strength, by having control of your attitude and thoughts, you and your family will benefit. Do not come down with the "poor-me syndrome." Everyone has the fire and desire within to succeed in every aspect of their life. Cultivate your strength by believing in the power of Determination, Perseverance and Endurance.

IT IS NOT MY FAULT!

I have had a very eventful life filled with sadness, madness and joy. I can smile now, but try telling the five year-old kid inside of me to smile. It's still hard for me to smile while revisiting my younger years. It's as if my life were caught up in a tornado, all of my thoughts going in circles and being tossed around in every direction. The physical, mental, and emotional pain was all very real. Even if this little kid stands cold-faced and fearless in front of me now, it wasn't always that way.

I do not seek to paint my mother as a bad or evil person. I know now that she did what she had to do to survive. She only had an 8th grade education and had made a series of poor choices, but ultimately she did what was best for me. I may not be happy about it because as a little kid I paid the price for her choices, whether good or bad. But I have to say I am happy with who I am today, and this in part allows me to forgive her.

I was born in the year 1970. I almost wasn't born though. My mother was married and had a daughter, my older sister, before she was divorced. She met my biological father and became pregnant with me. He was not happy that she was pregnant. She was a hardworking waitress trying to support her daughter and soon-to-be-born son. When she was seven months pregnant, my father came in to the diner where she worked and took her to the kitchen, where he beat her up. He kicked her in the stomach several times in an attempt to kill her unborn baby (me). He was yelling something about not wanting to have a kid. He was enraged that she planned to keep it. After that moment she feared for both her life and mine, and decided to hide from him.

I was born a healthy ten pound baby. I was just a big, pudgy kid. According to my mother I was born with a strong will, which became stronger as I grew into a toddler. It seems my willfulness was too much for her to handle, especially in light of the various insecurities in both her life and personality. Out of concern for my safety, she decided not to give me my father's last name for fear that he might one day find and kill me. She also decided to move from the town in which she was then living. But soon after I was born, my father did find us at her house, and threatened to kill me. She blocked his way to protect me, and he hit and kicked her. He then smashed the top off a beer bottle and held the sharp edge to my mother's throat. He said he would kill both of us.

I asked my Mom what attracted her to this monster,

and she said that he was charming, tall, and very good-looking. He was much older than her, loved music, and was a sergeant in the United States Army. He had served in World War II. She later heard from his parents that his sanity was affected after his tank was hit by artillery. He barely survived the explosion. He lived but those who knew him later said his mind sometimes didn't work right, and he often became very violent. There is some speculation that the war left him shell-shocked, or with Post Traumatic Stress Syndrome.

I realize that my mother did the best she possibly could, even though there were many mishaps. I know she was under a tremendous amount of stress having three different children from three different fathers. The financial burden left her wondering how she was going to pay for these kids. It must have been overwhelming. Sometimes people just want security and I believe this is what my mother finally found with my stepfather. Even though I loathed him as the primary reason for her getting rid of me, he did provide her and her newborn with a certain amount of stability.

I am not here to blame my mother, or to make her feel guilty for her "sins." We are all sinners. I no longer judge her or hold her accountable for the hell I went through. It is hard to forgive and move forward with one's life. But I have always moved forward, and that is why I am where I am in life. I am not, nor have I ever been, a drug addict, alcoholic, or convict. I could have taken the easy way out and played the victim, but I guarantee I would not be where I am today if I had taken that path.

I have done great things with my life, but I have always been troubled by questions that I needed to ask my mother. Why did you give me up and keep my brother and sister? Why did you hurt me? Why did you not come back for me? Why didn't you stay in touch with me more throughout my life? Where is my real father? Who is he? In the end, it was my county case files that finally provided the answers to these questions. Looking back, the questions weren't really as important as I thought they were. I made it through life without knowing the answers, and I turned out remarkably well compared to others in similar situations. But I dwelt on these questions for years because I felt the need to be validated, when in reality the only person that needed to validate me was me.

CHILD ABUSE
TRAPPED IN SAD MEMORIES

Child abuse is incomprehensibly hurtful and damaging to a child. I have been on the receiving end of child abuse and it has haunted me throughout my life. I'm not talking about a spanking once in a while. I am talking about inflicting severe pain on a child with the intent to cause physical trauma. I am talking about an out of control adult inflicting horrific pain on their own flesh and blood, a helpless little kid. Most mothers and fathers would do anything for their children, even die for them, but some soulless mothers and fathers are more than willing to hurt their kids mentally and physically.

I still remember very vividly one of the most horrific abuse incidents which ever happened to me. It is so embedded in my soul that it feels as if it just happened yesterday. I will take you there with me now.

It was a sunny day in California. The year was 1975. I was a kindergartner. I was a curious and tough five year-old boy. My mother, stepfather, half-brother, half-sister and I lived in a two story townhouse. There was nice green grass in front. When you walked inside, you saw the dining room and kitchen on the right and the family room on the left. In front of you was a staircase with a black iron banister leading to the bathroom and the bedrooms. The bathroom was located at the top of the stairs. The house was furnished and I remember the wood being very dark with big lamps made out of clear orange textured glass.

On the table and kitchen counter there would always be empty yellow Coors beer cans. I remember seeing lots of yellow Coors beer cans in those days.

I would often be outside playing in the tunnels under the main road overpass near our house. As a kid I called them tunnels but as an adult looking back, they were big storm drain pipes that went under the street. I am amazed that my Mom would let me wander and play over there at such a young age. I would love to hang out there and throw rocks at the metal siding of the pipes. When the rocks would hit, it would make a cool high-pitched noise that would echo through the tunnels. It would be exciting to sit under the overpass and hear the cars go honking by overhead. Sometimes I would find dead rats in there and lots of interesting junk. At times, adults would walk through, using the tunnels as a shortcut. Older kids would sometimes hang out in them. If I was alone, the tunnels would scare me a little, but I was tough and showed no fear.

One day, it was starting to get dark and I decided to head home. When I entered the townhouse, I could hear an argument going on between my mother and stepfather. I also remember a few yellow Coors beer cans. My mother asked me to do something. I defied her and said, "Screw you!" but really using the F-word. This wasn't the first time I had said these words to my mother. In fact the F-word was one of my favorite words at that age. But this time when I said it, my mother snapped, apparently having had enough of my disrespectful language. With anger in her eyes, she grabbed my arm and tried to pull me up the stairs. I resisted and fought back. I was yelling and she was yelling. It was very chaotic.

I was hitting her and she was hitting me, but eventually she overpowered me. She pulled me up the stairs to the bathroom and physically forced me to the sink. While holding me there, she turned on the hot water full blast, running it until the steam was rising. She kept yelling at me, screaming that I was never to use the F-word again, telling me how bad a kid I was. She emphasized this, how terrible I was, over and over again. I remember her yelling at me uncontrollably. I think she must have totally snapped.

What she did next was incomprehensible. She restrained my body and forced my tiny left hand under the scalding hot water.

I was screaming, out of control and trying to pull my hand out of the water. It hurt so much as she held it there. I screamed "Mommy stop, Mommy stop!" I was crying so loud, it hurt so much. I could not believe my own mother was doing this to me. It was like my life was flashing before my eyes and my whole body was shutting down. It was like she never heard me. I then yelled "Mommy, you're hurting me, it hurts mommy, let me go, I love you." I tried to get away but she looked at me with intense anger and said I was a bad kid. I thought I could get away, that I was stronger than her. But I couldn't. I was only five years old. I was helpless and completely at her mercy. The skin on the back of my left hand was burned off. I have had this scar ever since, on my body, in my heart, and in my mind.

All the other physical abuse I could deal with, but this particular incident altered me physically and mentally forever. This was the final ticker for the time bomb that was about to go off. I was no longer an innocent little boy. I was now overcome with a sense of shame and anger that would last for years. I realized I was no longer good enough and that I was not really loved. I felt worthless and unwanted.

I now hated my mother. I hated her for not sticking up for me, and for not loving me. I hated her for hurting me. I was her son. Hate is such a powerful word and I don't use it lightly, but if there are two people that I hated, it was my mother and stepfather. I can't say that I hated my biological father because I don't remember him, but my mother was supposed to protect and love me. I recently discovered from the case files on me that my biological father brutally abused me during my first year as a baby. Can you believe that? The wording is "Brutally abused." This was my biological father. How evil is that?

I stop here and ask God, "Why did you place me with this family?" Why God, are innocent children born into such terrible situations?" Born to drug-addicted parents, sexually abusive parents, physically abusive parents, and alcoholic parents. These people are so selfish! They can't think beyond themselves or realize how they are hurting and stunting the mental growth of their child. I can't stand the fact that they put themselves and their addictions before their children. If the cycle is not broken, each generation only gets worse.

There are too many distractions nowadays, pulling parents away from their children. These children don't have the good role models who could help them break the cycle. Most of them will become a product of their environment. It is unfortunate, but a good many parents don't deserve to be parents. They don't deserve to be the caretakers of Heaven's Angels. Each child is born pure and precious. They only want to be loved and they want to please their parents. They don't know negative feelings or words until their parents start showing them what a negative word or feeling means, and the child eventually mirrors the parent's example. Everything you do or don't do with your kid molds them. What was once a pure and precious little angel can turn into an uncontrollable and aggressive little monster. I know this because my mother thought I was a devil. Sons and daughters want and deserve love from their mother and father no matter what. It doesn't matter how mean their parents are. They just want attention and love. Even as children grow into adults, they still yearn for the love and approval of their parents. I always wanted and desired my mother's love. Even as an adult, I just wanted to be validated by her.

Let's face it, I was a mistake. I was never supposed to be born. I'm sure my mother was frustrated when she accidentally became pregnant by a man who had so many emotional problems, a history of violence, who was a thief and convicted felon. Now I understand people can change for the better after making bad choices, but only IF THEY WANT TO. It appears that my biological father was never going to learn and was doomed to be a loser. My mother had to be frustrated for putting herself in that situation, and was unable to live with the consequences: me. I felt that I was a mistake, and that she was going to make me pay for it every time I behaved badly. I couldn't believe my own mother would hurt me as badly as she did, or be so vindictive.

I remember the pain. I feel the pain. I smell the pain and I see the pain. Never will I forget the memory of what was done to that innocent little five year-old boy. It is difficult to really describe the feeling of the hot scalding water burning off the majority of the skin on the top of my left hand. You could literally pull off parts of my flesh. It was awful!

I remember how angry my mother was. I wondered why I received this new kind of punishment. I kept asking, "Why has my Mom hurt me so bad?" I remember looking up at my Mom and seeing her reflection in the mirror, the intense look that was there. She was so focused on hurting me and taking out all of her frustration. No wonder I was diagnosed as emotionally disturbed or a "bad kid." I was a product of my environment.

This particular abusive event has followed me throughout my life. It has literally haunted me every time I take a shower. Before I get into the shower, I'll test the water with my hand to make sure it isn't too hot. Every time I touch the water, it automatically takes me back to the moment when my mother held my hand under the scalding water. It was uncontrollable. I could not block it out of my mind. I just lived it over and over every day of my life. It was like a broken record, constantly repeating over and over again. I had to make sure the water wasn't hot. I would look at my left hand and remember the skin burnt off and the pink color that showed beneath.

I would also recall this horrific event every time I washed dishes, got into a hot tub, or washed my hands. If the water even had the possibility of being hot, I would recall the awful memory of being burned. I have thought about what my mother did to me every single day of my life, ever since the day it occurred.

I believe this was the greatest obstacle to me attaining complete happiness with myself at an early age. This unhappiness followed me everywhere. Anger would flow through my heart, then sadness. Every day I had to relive that experience, and it would put me in a negative frame of mind. If I could not get over it quickly enough, this negativity would color my entire day, affecting others around me.

As a child and teenager I tried many different forms of therapy. But there is one particular kind of therapy which worked amazingly well in ridding me of the fear of hot water. I highly recommend it to others. It is called EMDR (Eye Movement and Desensitization and Reprocessing) Website: www.emdria.org

Another unfortunate event happened to me when I was about five years old. I sometimes had a problem wetting my bed. Or if I was mad at my parents I would pee on their things. That was my way of telling them I didn't want to be treated the way they were treating me. If I wet my bed the night before, my stepfather would become very angry with me. So he'd pull me over to the toilet and force my head into the bowl. He would stand over me and push my head down, forcing me to stay there. Now I didn't ever come close to drowning, but it wasn't a nice thing to do to another human being. He was treating me like a misbehaving dog or animal. He probably considered me an animal. He did not like me. I was the middle child, putting major pressure and stress on his marriage to my mother. He had his own son, the youngest, and I was now the bad seed. I'm sure he was nice to me in the beginning, at least until he won my Mom over.

Well this one time when he was sticking my head into the toilet, my mother heard the commotion. He was yelling at me about peeing my bed, telling me how angry he was. My Mom told him to stop holding my head down. There was a huge argument, and in the heat of it all, as he was forcing my head into the toilet, she grabbed my left hand and yanked my arm back. She yanked it so hard that she caused shoulder damage. I cannot tell you if it was dislocated, or if something was ripped or broken, but it was so painful that she made me a sling to hold my arm up. Years later, I still have pain in my shoulder, and it always rests higher than the other one. Every morning I have to try and force my bad shoulder down and stretch it out so that it's comfortable throughout the day.

At least after that day, my stepfather stopped putting my head in the toilet.

Abuse is hard to live with, but fortunately I am a fighter. I am a conqueror who has set his mind free. Life isn't fair. The only thing I can control is my attitude and outlook on it. My philosophy and motto are simple: I WILL NEVER GIVE UP!

DON'T LEAVE ME MOM!

Here I was, a child desperate for love and affection, a scared little boy who was getting ready for what would be the longest ride of his life. I can't say I remember the drive to the orphanage, or the place where kids were stored, but I do remember not bringing along any toys. I remember the sun being out and the sky being blue. The day was pleasant, warm, and peaceful, in stark contrast to the foreboding anxieties that were raging inside me. I didn't know where I was being taken, only that this day would likely be the darkest of my life. The "longest ride" eventually ended at a place I considered an orphanage. It was a big building with lots of space and rooms. I figured it was an orphanage because all I saw were homeless and unloved kids. Kids who were no longer wanted by their Moms and Dads. I could see the sadness and fear in their eyes, and imagined that same fear must be showing in mine. We were now disposable, kids who could be thrown away or tossed overboard, never to be loved or comforted by our parents again.

Seriously, who would have cared if we were drowned or burned to death? At this point, it was already like we were being buried alive. We were being killed, suffocated, by lack of love. We were now the county's worry, pain and nightmare. My parents had given up! They were weak, and now I had to somehow become strong and survive. I felt deep misgivings and anxiety, the memories were killing me. I kept thinking, 'Where is my big sister?' I thought that surely she would come and rescue me because she loved me. I expected her to show up at any minute. But nobody came! Here I was, a help-less little five year-old boy, and my heart no longer beat for anybody but myself. Hope was lost for me at that point.

I don't even remember seeing my mother's eyes, or her giving me one final hug, or her even saying something as simple as "I love you Derek," or, "I will be back for you son." How could she not even give me a goodbye hug? She was the one who had placed both herself and me in this position.

I was the son, paying the price for all of her bad choices. She could have at least said, "Well, take care Derek, I love you." Or how about just a few basic words of tenderness and encouragement? "You will make it through this Derek." Even some-thing negative, critical, or hurtful would have been better than nothing: "I blame you for all of this," or "Derek, you are the devil," or "Derek, I hate you for what you have become," or "Derek, you forced me to do this, I blame you!" But NO, nothing was said, and the indifferent silence was more painful than any words could have been, no matter how angry or loveless.

I guess it wasn't like she was wishing me well as I went off to college. I'm sure she quickly got rid of me in order to avoid the emotional impact of her actions, of seeing herself throwing away her own blood, her selfish desire to choose her husband over me, her son. But as her blood son, I probably reminded her of past mistakes, of the regretful choice she made to start a romantic relationship with my biological father. I have no doubt my stepfather comforted her, and told her she was making the right choice in giving her son away. Even as a little boy, I was certain he had been the one pushing to give me away. He was a piece of crap! No doubt he still is today. He broke up our family. I hoped that every day after he gave up me he lived a life of hell, and that when he died, hell would take him back. My Mom used to call me the devil, but as far as I could see, she'd married the devil. She got it all mixed up. Mother, you married the devil.

After she dropped me off, my little life as a boy who nobody could or would love began. At this time, I wasn't even able to love this little boy. Plagued with insecurities and doubts about my self-worth, I was now going to have to make a home here in hell. I was left alone with all the bigger boys, who just stared at me like wolves salivating at their thoughts of feasting on a weak, vulnerable little lamb. I was the proverbial sheep being lead to the slaughter. I was very alert and very scared. Very, very, very scared!

A woman took me into another room and showed me around. It technically wasn't an orphanage, but there was very little difference between an orphanage and whatever this place was. Besides, what difference did it make? It was an imposing, overwhelming, cold, impersonal and institutional building. There was no love here. This was a place of pain and ghosts. We were throwaways or misfits. Possibly we were angels who nobody recognized as such, but that could hardly have occurred to us at the time. This was to be my new home while a new family was being prepared for me. I didn't know who or what kind of people might invite me to share in their life. Or for that matter, if anybody would want me at all.

I remember thinking that my Mom would of course be coming back for me. I could care less about my stepfather, but I trusted that my mother's love would override whatever other concerns she had. I felt a deep hatred for my stepfather. He had taken my Mom away from me. If she didn't come back, I placed the blame squarely on his shoulders. I cried from loneliness and fear. The older boys were antagonizing and threatening me, trying to push my limits.

I got angry and taunted them back, so one of the boys pulled out a toothbrush with the end sharpened for use as a weapon. I ran for my life. I thought I was going to die. I knew what death was even at a young age. According to the county reports I had a kind of morbid fascination with death. Later that night, when it got dark, I grew even more frightened. It became obvious that if my mother was going to come back for me, it wouldn't be any time soon.

We slept in what appeared to me like a giant classroom with a bunch of beds placed in it. It was some kind of enormous warehouse for storing kids. I remember hearing lots of crying in the middle of the night, puncturing through the silence. Other kids were missing their Moms and Dads, brother and sisters. Where were mine? I wondered why my brother and sister got to stay with our mother and I was stuck here in this sad, terrible place. Why was I rejected and deleted from the family? Was I special somehow, or was I just a piece of garbage? Why couldn't I just be a normal kid like others? A kid who had a family? Why didn't anyone love me? Why couldn't I just be a kid?

MY LIFE AS A 5 YEAR-OLD, THROUGH THE EYES OF AN ADULT

When I was five years-old it was a crazy time for me. I figure instead of trying to recall everything and explain my behavior in my own words, I prefer to let the adults in my life paint the picture of what was going on. This is just one of the reports which labeled and diagnosed me. Additional reports are in the appendix at the back of the book. They are the reports which decided my fate, but my fate was destined to be different than what their diagnoses implied. This information is very revealing about my childhood. It should be understood that I was a product of my environment. All I wanted was to be a kid and be with my family. All of a sudden I was getting diagnosed and mentally picked apart like some lab monkey or diseased mouse. I felt like a medical experiment.

When you read these, you will see that I was just a little boy who was very conscious of what was going on. After I first read these reports, I was very sorry for that little boy who they were diagnosing, trying to get inside his head. It took a couple of days for me to get over the sadness I felt for him. I could not believe this little boy was me. I have four little children of my own, and can't imagine having people pick them apart in order to ascertain where they should be placed in the world, all according to impersonal professional standards.

For those who have a child, try visualizing him or her at five years old in a similar situation. A situation in which he or she feels completely alone, unsafe, unprotected, and Mommy or Daddy are not there to comfort. I remember some of these evaluations and how I behaved.

I am a fighter by nature and early on showed signs of stubbornness in doing what I wanted and refusing to acknowledge another's opinion of me. This tendency has carried on throughout my life. I do everything "Derek's way." I felt like the world was against me and that nobody liked me. I felt like I was totally backed into a corner, and the only way for me to let others know I was a real kid was to come out swinging.

Derek's Way may not always be the quickest or best way, but it's an eventful and adventurous way, and it has gotten me to the point in life where I am now. I love the place where the road of life has finally brought me. What a great destination. I believe my past was instrumental in bringing me to this moment, where I enjoy who I am and live a life full of enthusiasm. What you are about to read is the real deal.

REPORT FOR THE COUNTY JUVENILE COURT

July 8, 1976

The mother describes Derek's father as an ex-convict and an alcoholic, with severe emotional problems. The mother lost contact with Derek's father soon after the child's birth, but believes he returned to prison shortly thereafter for involvement in several armed robberies.

PSYCHOLOGICAL INFORMATION:

A verbal report from the doctor states that while the boy is not overtly psychotic, there is indication of this potential. The child laughs inappropriately and shows great anxiety. He is very suspicious of people and holds back as if fearful of making a mistake. Derek reminds his mother of his father and this causes her to reject Derek in many ways.

He needs further testing to more accurately determine his I.Q. **He does not recognize such words as "dog, boy, cat."**

PARENTS STATEMENT:

After being advised of their rights, Derek's mother and stepfather stated that the minor has experienced emotional problems since the age of eighteen months. They stated that during the past year the minor's behavior has grown virtually unmanageable at times. They stated that he was unable to finish his kindergarten year in school because of problems he experienced with the other children and the disruptive behavior he demonstrated.

The parents state that the boy is hyperactive and that when he becomes involved in an activity which might endanger him or others around him, he will not respond to reasonable directions to stop this negative type of behavior. The parents further state that the minor must be physically restrained, and that he frequently flies into rages and is completely unmanageable.

On more than one occasion in the past year, the minor has been observed to pound his head on the floor. The parents further state that they cannot tolerate this behavior and the mother is fearful of hitting the child and injuring him. The stepfather states that the minor will not respond to his directions nor will the minor respond to the directions of the older sibling in the home. The parents believe that the minor must be supervised closely at all times and they are not capable of this level of supervision. At the present time, the parents have indicated that they are "unwilling" to participate in a program of counseling because they do not believe counseling will help solve the minor's behavior problem. The parent's were referred to this agency by the Psychiatric Emergency Unit.

PLACEMENT PLANS:

Emergency Foster Home Mother states that Derek is more physically aggressive than other children. She states that Derek is affectionate. Derek first went to the Emergency Foster Home on June 18th, 1976 and has remained there except for an eight day period when he returned to his parent's care. A sense of affection has developed between Derek and his Foster Parents.

FATHER:

Derek's father's whereabouts are unknown. He has not seen Derek since Derek was nine months old. **The last information the mother had on the father was that he was in an institution for the criminally insane.**

MOTHER AND STEPFATHER:

Mother and stepfather continue to have problems that make it difficult for them to deal with Derek. Mother does not show an ability to deal with or help resolve Derek's problems. Stepfather has mainly felt that the problems experienced were Derek's and not his. He was not willing to participate in therapy.
In considering whether or not Derek should return home, his decision was based on whether Derek has changed.

Since the jurisdictional court hearing, the mother and stepfather were originally planning on Derek's returning home after the school year. They saw out of home placement as a temporary plan to give Derek time to change his unmanageable behavior, and to give them time to consider how they might better deal with Derek. However in March, 1977 they decided they were unable to consider Derek's return. They felt, based on Derek's behavior during their visits, that he had not changed and they were unable to cope with his behavior. The parents appear to have very little willingness to use any counseling resources. They also declined the suggestion of parenting classes.

As an alternative to family restoration, they requested Derek be referred for adoption. However, the adoptions department was unable to accept this referral based on the severity of Derek's emotional problems. Guardianship was suggested as an alternative plan and the parents were in agreement. Following their decision, they have chosen not to visit Derek.

Derek:

Derek is described as a child with emotional problems. Neurological, psychological and learning disability evaluations were done on Derek. **Neurological tests indicate he is functioning on a normal 2 ? to 4 year old level, they indicate "mild retardation".** The psychological examination done for the Learning Disability Evaluation diagnose Derek as having Aretic Psychosis. It appears many of these problems are associated with his family. Both foster homes have reported problems with Derek's encopretic and eneuretic behavior, but this behavior is noticed only occasionally when Derek is under stress. The current foster family reports that Derek's behavior was the most difficult to deal with during the time the parents were visiting. Derek seems to accept not returning to his mother's home and remaining with the foster family. He does ask about his mother and asks for visits with her but has not asked about returning home.

PLACEMENT REVIEW:

Special placement problems are hyperactive, emotionally disturbed youngster. **Neurological tests
indicate "mild retardation".** Derek is having diffi-
culty adjusting to school. Although he has adjusted
well to this emergency foster home, the foster mother reports he gets upset by the other foster children
leaving.

WORDS THAT KILL THE SPIRIT

As you can see from the reports, a lot of effort was put into describing my personality and mental capacity. One of the most disturbing words the doctor used was "retarded." I believe that this word, along with loser, stupid, and dumb, are some of the most damaging words in the English language. These words are extremely harmful to kids. What we think we can become, we usually can become. I believe labeling a child can become a self-fulfilling prophecy. If a child is constantly getting cut down and labeled, I believe he will lose the will to try and become something better than expected.

These hurtful words do not uplift children. They are meant to demoralize them and make them feel like lesser beings. Even when kids joke about being a "retard" or say "I am dumb," or, "You are stupid," it gradually instills that negativity in their minds. The result is that oftentimes kids will grow to fit that label. Their mental hard drive is being programmed, and these labels and words may never be erased. If you assimilate these limiting, destructive words, you may start believing what they imply.

And if everyone else believes in their accuracy, it can

lead to various forms of self-destruction. You can see it in kids suffering from low self-esteem and lack of confidence. They just might be living up to a label somebody else has applied to them. What labels have you allowed to characterize yourself or your children? This labeling could have damaging effects throughout their life.

Yes, I had slowness in development and yes, I had a lot of emotional problems. But if everyone hastily slaps a label on a child, he or she will eventually live up to that characterization. How can somebody grow if it's already assumed their growth is stunted? This applies not only to children of all ages, but adults as well. We all need positive reinforcement. Don't let anyone's thoughts identify you and tell you what your limits are. Don't let anyone design you and fill your head with doubt. Stand up proud and determined to become the sole architect of your mind and soul. You are the master of your own mind.

If I had known how I was labeled as a child, I know I would have turned out very differently, and would possibly be in prison or even dead. Don't let anyone use a label to turn you into something you are not.

I dislike the word "retarded." I believe mentally-challenged children are angels sent from Heaven to teach us the virtues of love, appreciation, sacrifice and selflessness. I have more respect for mentally-challenged people who overcome great obstacles than "normal, high-achieving" individuals. These special, mentally-challenged individuals are a gift. They are great teachers. We can all learn from them. Anyone with a disability is here to enrich our lives. Respect them, watch and listen to them. Even though some are unable to speak, we can still learn a lot from their silence. We are all connected as human beings. If your soul is open, it will allow you to see the little miracles working throughout our daily lives in mysterious ways.

A NEW FOSTER HOME
ON A FARM

Here is a paper I found in my journal from my teenage years as a foster kid. I wrote about my experience living on a farm with lots of animals. I love animals and the spirit of healing they bring to us. Animals are so in tune to the human spirit. As a foster child, they helped me learn how to love again when I felt no one loved me. Horses are an amazing animal with feelings that can sense our sadness. As animals, they have unique abilities to teach by example, how to love unconditionally, and how to heal the spirit of a wounded child.

"As I lay in my hammock swinging in a grove of eucalyptus trees, the clean, fresh, sinus-cleaning scent sifts through my nose and I am able to reminisce about some of my greatest memories. They are still so vivid, and will be forever. Who can ever forget the combined smell of corn husks, pine and eucalyptus trees, beautiful flowers and roses touched off with the sounds and odors of our farm animals? The smell of horse and goat manure used as fertilizer for the plants is drowned out by the sweet aroma of the beautiful flowers and the roses which attract honeybees. On the other hand, the manure attracts the flies. What a small price to pay for the setting of beautiful memories!

"I remember the early mornings. I would have to wake up and go into the horse pasture and help my dad shovel horse manure into the pickup truck. That was easy compared to going into the goat pen and carrying out loaded buckets and garbage cans full of goat manure. The main problem was that the pen was not a flat piece of land, it was at a tilt. So it was a little harder to carry the buckets out. Sometimes my parents would pay me twenty-five cents for each bucket I filled. Getting paid was nice, but I also enjoyed the fruits of my labor when eating fresh apples, zucchini, corn, string beans, cantaloupes, squash, broccoli and tomatoes.

"There's nothing like biting into a fresh cob of corn and having the kernels pop as you chomp down. Then there were the good old family picnics where we would all saddle up our horses and ride to Garin Ranch and partake of hamburgers, hotdogs, Jell-O, and cookies.

"My foster Mom would usually drive the car to the park and meet us there in order to have the hamburgers ready when we rode in starving for food. The ride was about two hours and the horses were grateful for the break as we ate.

At home I was responsible for breaking in (training) one of our ponies. His name was Bootie, an American white pony, very large and ready to take anybody for the wild ride of their life.

"I calmed him down after getting bucked off

several times. It takes a lot of courage for a young boy to get back on a pony after being bucked off. Now he is a fast, smooth and well-disciplined ride.

"In the early morning I would get up and milk the goats. We had five that were milking and they would give about two-and-a-half gallons total. After milking, I would come into the house and filter the milk, put the date on the bottle and refrigerate it. Any effort was worth some fresh goat milk. I loved having a fresh glass of goat milk with chocolate chip cookies.

" I come from a foster family of seven kids and sometimes there would be a few extra foster children. I think my mother and father's door is always open for a lost kid who needs good, loving parents. The atmosphere when I walk into my house is cheerful, with the helping hand of Mom and Dad.

"Materially, the furniture is beat down, the carpet has been trod on over a million and a half times. The kitchen table is large enough for an army. There are toys lying around for people to walk on and break. It is not as clean as other people's houses, but what can you expect when you come from a large family who rides horseback, takes care of farm animals, plays in acres of dirt, goes dirt-bike riding, builds massive forts, climbs trees, and takes apart greasy motor parts. After all this we come into the house and sit down. One just can't have classy, expensive stuff when they live like that.

"I wouldn't give up this place for anything,

because we as a family have made this house our home, full of love and closeness. Special family ties have been made that will never be broken. There are too many memories to recall on paper, but I can say one thing: a home like this makes the grouchiest people smile because it's a true fairy-land."

AN ANGRY KID

Here is a journal entry from a talk I gave in church when I was twelve years old.

"I have a goal. I am working on becoming more like Jesus. One of my problems is losing my temper. When a person gets mad and loses control of himself, bad things often happen.

"Lots of times we have to decide if we are going to let people or things make us lose control of ourselves. We do have the power to decide whether we will let ourselves become angry or not.

"When we get mad at our brother or sister, we act differently than when we get mad at our parents or teachers. You don't hit your teachers or parents, but brothers and sisters are often fair game.

"When I was about eight years old, I started getting warts on my hands. Now these weren't little warts. They were big warts. They just got bigger and bigger. It was crazy and embarrassing. I hated them. Kids at school used to make me mad when they would call me "Wartman". They would see me coming and say "Oh, here comes the Wartman". I couldn't help it. I went to the doctor and every time they burned one off, a bigger one took its place. At one time, I had over 100 of the ugly things. I used to get mad and lose my temper and do terrible things and end up getting a detention. I would have to stay after school and that made me madder.

"Several years ago, I got mad at my older brother Colin when he was wrestling with me. He hurt me so I took revenge and punched a hole in his fish tank and cut my arm very badly. It was a bloody mess. I had cut a blood artery. Blood was spurting out like crazy. It was like a geyser. It was a mess for a long time and meant that I couldn't do a lot of fun things that summer.

"Then last year I got into a fight with a kid at school. He kept bugging me and bugging me until I got so mad that I broke a school window. I had to pay for it and it wasn't cheap.

"I was a little lucky because the Principal Mr. Cox let me work it off by helping the janitor clean up the school. I hate to clean toilets.

"I know God loves me and trusts me. I know that to honor God, I must learn to control myself. I have to learn to act as Jesus would act. He would never let other people make him lose his temper. I must learn to be like him. Life goes better when we try our best to be like Jesus."

Here is another journal entry from when I was 10 years old.

"Have you ever witnessed a geyser of blood squirting from your body similar to the water geysers squirting in Yellowstone National Park? I'm here to tell you it was one of the scariest times of my life.

"It was the early summer of 1980 and my older brother Colin and I were in the front yard doing our chores. My chore at the time was sweeping our huge driveway while Colin was cleaning his fish tank, in which he kept snakes. Colin took pride in showing friends the large King Snake he had caught while on a hike.

"Do you know that saying, 'one boy, one brain; two boys, half a brain; and three boys, no brain at all'? Well, while Mom and Dad were in the house not looking, I would horse around and tease my older brother. Eventually coming to the end of his endurance, it was time for him to exercise some discipline on his psycho little brother, me.

"We started punching and kicking, eventually wrestling on the driveway. When we were finished with our match, I decided I was going to get the last kick in. So when he wasn't paying attention, I aimed a kick at his face. The kick was going smoothly until he caught my foot in mid-air. Unbalanced, I fell to the ground.

"Talk about being ticked off! I was in an uproar. I wanted to get him back big time, so with no hesitation I walked to his snake tank and hit it so hard my hand went crashing through the glass. Reflexively, I yanked my hand out and naturally cut my wrist very deeply, all the way down to the main blood vein.

"I didn't know it was deep until a geyser of blood was squirting about a foot high off my wrist. My brother and I were amazed. I panicked like a chicken with its head cut off.

"I remember screaming and running for Mom. I ran inside the house, blood squirting all over the walls, looking for my mother. I found her, and she quickly got a towel and applied direct pressure. She was as scared as I was. I was screaming, thinking I was surely a goner.

"We got into the car, drove to the hospital, and demanded medical attention right then and there. The doctor said I cut my main artery by forcefully yanking my arm into the glass that was still intact as I pulled it out of the snake tank.
It cut my flesh deeper.

"I will never forget being so scared, thinking that I was going to die. I was sure I'd bleed to death. Later that summer I paid the consequences for my behavior when our family went camping at a lake. I had to sit out and watch everybody swim while I tried not to get my cut infected. It was a long uneventful summer. The open wound took three months to heal, while everybody else was playing. I was just thankful to be alive. I learned a valuable lesson that year: there are consequences for your actions, and sometimes you pay more dearly than at other times."

Here is another example:

"Drills can be a weapon as well as a very useful tool. It was a nice morning in the year of 1982 and I had nothing better to do than pester my older brother and his friend while they fixed their car. My brother had told me to get way from them before I got hurt. I took that as a challenge, and so started to really bug him. When someone bugs you for awhile, they grow impatient, and that's exactly what he did. He came after me, but my quickness exceeded his.

"Huh..." I thought, "I am going to bug him again!" His friend threatened to use the drill in his hand and drill me to bits. Well, what did I do? I ran right towards him, screaming "Drill me!"

"Sure enough, I ran right into the drill as it was turning, and it drilled right into my upper leg about a quarter of an inch. It hurt! What was I thinking, doing that? I had accepted the challenge of defeating my brother and his friend, and once again I paid the consequences for my actions."

CRAZY STORIES
OF UNCONDITIONAL LOVE

I AM SO FORTUNATE TO HAVE HAD FOSTER PARENTS WHO NEVER GAVE UP ON ME. My foster parents are very special to me, although being the hell-raiser I was it wasn't always obvious. I DO CONSIDER THEM MY MOM AND DAD. THEY HAVE EARNED IT! I have an undying gratitude for what they did for me. They were both schoolteachers and devoted their time to helping me grow, both mentally and emotionally. Their love for children was expressed in the size of the family they had. When I joined, there were five children. Later on it became a family of nine, including their own kids and other long-term foster children.

They were extremely patient and they loved me unconditionally. But, man!—I was constantly testing the limits of that unconditional love. No doubt it was tested to the extreme. They had to put up with much that average parents may not have to. They are saints. They have done their duty with love, and have paid the price to have me call them Mom and Dad. I was definitely a handful, and they had to endure far more than what was expected of them as foster parents. They were very tolerant. Ask yourself, would you have kept me as a foster kid after reading the following little stories?

Here are a few short stories about what they had to deal with. Some are very serious. I don't consider many of the events I'm going to tell about very funny. I don't take them lightly. This was serious stuff, and my bad choices often impacted others in negative ways. I am very sorry to the individuals who I hurt in the past. I am merely sharing with you a few examples of what I put my foster parents through. This will give you a feel for my personality and behavior at that time.

Here we go, this is some real stuff.

As a young boy I had a fascination with knives and guns. I would always fantasize about cutting people with a knife. From the normal person's point of view, I was a pretty twisted little boy. When I was about seven years old I found a razor blade, and started to carry it around in my pocket. One day when my neighborhood friend, about three years younger than I, would not do what I said, I took out my razor blade and threatened him. I wanted him to go down the hill on his Big-Wheel. Razor blade held out threateningly, I told him that if he didn't go down the hill on his Big-Wheel, I'd cut him.

Well he didn't go down the hill because he was scared to. It was a big hill. As I was yelling and swiping the air in front of him with the razor blade, he got very frightened. Trying to protect himself, he stretched his hands out to shield his body, and I proceeded to purposely cut his hand with the blade. It cut through the webbing of skin between the thumb and first finger. The cut went completely down to the bone. Blood was flowing everywhere. He ran screaming all the way home. I then went home and didn't tell anyone about the incident, wishing it would just go away. Soon after, the Dad next door called my Dad, and then all hell broke loose. They wanted to talk with me and my father when they returned from the emergency room.

When they finally got back and we went over to their house, my friend's Dad was so angry with me that he wanted to do the punishing. He wanted to give me a hard spanking. My Mom and Dad were extremely upset over me taking my stabbing fantasy out on a neighbor boy. I felt terrible too, and knew I was going to be in big-time trouble with the county and my social worker. This event pretty well cured me of my fascination with knives.

Thank goodness I never killed anyone. I ran into my neighborhood friend a couple years back at a motor-cycle shop. We are now in our 30's, and he'd heard that my music was starting to get noticed. He told me if I ever make it big time, he's going to get his scar tattooed. He showed me the old scar and it was quite big. I wish it had never happened. I am so sorry for doing what I did, and I deeply thank him for forgiving me.

On to a much different story; one not quite as violent.

Living on the farm, I had many opportunities to find insects and play with them. There was one insect in particular abundance, and there were always tons of them crawling around under boards and logs. These were pincher bugs. They are little bugs, about half an inch long, with big ugly pinchers.

There were dozens, if not hundreds or thousands of pincher colonies on the property. One day I had just finished the last of my Tic-Tac breath mints, and decided to use the empty container as an insect box. So I scooped up lots of pincher bugs, stuffing them in until the clear little box was almost full to capacity. The container was perfect for me, because I could just carry all the insects around in my pocket and they'd never get out. I was now like a walking insect aquarium.

My parents knew about my little insect collection. They didn't know, however, that I took the Tic-Tac container with me to school one day so I could show my classmates all my cool bugs. At recess I was hanging out with some friends, and a few of the girls were teasing me. I told them to stop but they wouldn't. It made me mad so I took out the Tic-Tac container, opened it up, and shook it wildly in the air in order to spray them with bugs. The pincher bugs were flying out of the container and into the girls' hair. I was so busted. Everything got chaotic from there, and I was called into the principal's office and suspended from school.

I got suspended a lot in elementary school, mostly for fighting. One of the crazier times at school was in the fourth grade, when I started a gang called the Hell's Angels Juniors. Every morning at the baseball field, my three friends and I would take black felt-tip pens and "tattoo" the words "Hell's Angels Juniors" on our upper arms so we could hide it from teachers and parents.

I don't know how I knew about Hell's Angels at that time, but I knew I wanted to belong to something big. A bad, tough motorcycle gang seemed perfect for me. For the record, I am not a Hell's Angel.

I remember at that time there was a lot of trouble between what were called High Riders and Low Riders. I considered myself a High Rider. I got in lots of fights as a High Rider, and was suspended several times. While in fourth grade I got into a fight with a Low Rider and he knocked my tooth out. I was so mad. I'd been beaten up. We got him back later by scaring the crap out of him. He later became my friend for the rest of the school year. But the following year he went on to junior high and I was now a fifth grader. As a fifth grader I was now considered "King of the School," meaning that nobody would take me on in a fight or disrespect me. I had proven myself as a fighter and a force not to be messed with.

I had a system going on in elementary school. It was quite elaborate for a kid my age. When the bus would drop me off in front of school, I wouldn't go in. Instead, I ran down the street, taking a side road over the hill to the candy shop. When I was done buying candy I would come back to school and be marked tardy. But I had my stash of candy in a brown paper bag, so I was happy.

I would also cut school during recess or the lunch hour just to get to the candy store. At recess I would have a friend in my gang distract the yard-duty supervisor at the tether-ball poles so a buddy of mine and I could slip out the back gate. We ran as fast as we could to make it to the candy store and back by the time the bell rang for class. We'd buy Jolly Rancher Stix and Now-and-Later candies for a nickel a piece, then sell them on the playground for a quarter. After a while, I no longer ditched to buy candy. Instead, I would recruit runners and they'd ditch recess to bring the candy stash back to me.

Soon my friend and I decided to take things a step further, so we ditched lunch to go for a hamburger. The fast food place was pretty far away but we made it. On the way back, while we were walking up the hill, I saw my Dad's orange VW Bug coming up behind us. I could have seen that bright orange car coming from a mile away. I was freaking out. I told my friend that I just saw my Dad's car, and urged him to remain calm. I had to look calm, cool and collected in front of my friend, so I just said to keep going up the hill and look straight ahead.

Whatever he did, he was not to look at the cars going by. The orange VW went by up the hill. 'Whew...I'm safe,' I thought. But my Dad must have seen us in the rear-view mirror, because he stopped his car right then and there. I told my friend to run, but he didn't. I knew I'd been caught. My Dad waited for us to walk by the car. He asked what we were doing out of school. I told him we were hungry, so we left. We got into the car. He drove us back to school and brought us to the principal's office. I remember getting a lot of detentions because of that. Thanks for ratting us out, Dad!

Another fun adventure that got me into a lot of trouble was a time when my Dad was at the police station taking care of a ticket. I must have been around twelve years old. He had me wait in the truck while he took care of the issue. After waiting a while, I was beginning to get bored, so I got out of the truck and saw a few nails on the floorboard. I grabbed them and put them in my pocket. I looked around the parking lot at all the cars. I decided that I wanted to have a little fun, so I walked around looking for intriguing vehicles and let the air out of their tires. I used the tip of the nail to push in the tire valve, letting the air out. It was fun because I got to sneak around. I was popping my head out from behind one of the cars when I saw the big prize, a bunch of police cars parked in a gated lot. The gate happened to be open. I took the chance and crept right through it.

I felt like a highly trained soldier, making myself invisible. I hid behind one of the police cruisers and took a glance around the premises to see if there was anybody around. It was clear, so I proceeded to let the air out of the tires. I also set some nails up in front of the tires so that when the police officer drove out he or she would roll over them and get their tires punctured. I did this to a few cars, when all of a sudden I saw policemen coming out the rear door of the building, running towards me. I tried to hide, but it was too late. They grabbed me and brought me inside. They sat me down in an office and held me there. I told them I was here with my Dad. I asked one of the policeman, "How did you catch me?" He said there were cameras stationed all over the building. They notified my Dad and he came to get me. I was in big trouble and my Dad was terribly embarrassed.

The police let me go with a strong warning. My Dad, on the other hand, put me to a lot of hard work on the farm and placed me on "restriction." I guess that was better than juvenile hall.

One of my favorite idiotic times occurred when I was returning to school from an early morning church event. A senior in high school let my friends and me catch a ride with him back to school. What he didn't know was that I was thinking very mischievous thoughts, and had plans to give him a good scare. My friends and I were sitting in the back seats of his big van. There were side windows, but they only opened up a little. Just enough to throw jumping jacks out of.

Jumping jacks are as big as firecrackers, but when ignited they jump and spin, letting off sparks and a loud crackling sound. I had a ton of these things. I would light the jumping jacks and throw them out the window at people walking or jogging on the streets. The driver didn't notice a thing. When we got to school, we thanked him for the ride. But before we left I opened up the front passenger door, lit two jumping jacks and threw them at him. He was in shock! My friends were in shock! I wanted to show my friends that I wasn't scared of doing anything. They landed on him but eventually fell down at his feet by the pedals. They were spinning and jumping around the gas and brake pedals. He was kicking his feet and screaming in a panic while I was laughing and getting a big kick out of it. My friends were totally scared for me then.

After the fireworks had stopped he was so mad that he got out of the van and came over to give me a hard punch in the chest. He was a senior in high school and I was a freshman—a big difference in age and size. I took the punch like a man. He was yelling at me and said he was going to tell my Mom and Dad. Now I was the one who was scared! I didn't show it though. I left with my friends and went to class, but I couldn't help thinking how busted I was going to be when I got home. I was really worried. As the day went by, I happened to see the senior and went up to him while nobody was looking and told him how sorry I was and to please not tell my parents. He told me he'd think about it. He could tell how scared I was. I was no longer that bulletproof little freshman he'd seen earlier that morning. He now saw the vulnerable and frightened freshman. He made me suffer for the rest of the day. I went home without knowing whether he'd told my parents what had happened.

They didn't bring it up that night. I saw him again at school the next day and he promised not to tell my parents. I told him, "Thank you so much for letting me live another day." I was never mean to that guy again.

Now what do you think of when you think of a Boy Scout? Do you think of good little boys who want to help out others and are always prepared? Well that wasn't me when I was a Scout. I joined the Boy Scouts because it was mandatory in my family. I don't regret it. It was a lot of fun. But I didn't live up to the example that Boy Scouts are supposed to portray. Call me a Wild Scout hanging out with a bunch of boys. I enjoyed all the camping and special activities, but I wasn't too fond of participating in the community service projects.

At least I can claim to have never had a problem with cheating or dishonesty. That was one very important thing I had going, and that I am still proud of. I am happy that honesty was a major part of my character, but I did have other problems. I would not respect authority or the older Boy Scouts. At Scout Camp, I got into countless fights with a few of the older members. I definitely pushed the limits. I was not considered a leader, nor was I considered a particularly good example to the rest of the troop. I had a potty mouth, was constantly instigating trouble, and I refused to do things any way but my own. I always wanted to get attention, even if it was the wrong type of attention.

My parents had a rule in our family which had it that boys could not get their driver's license until they had earned the rank of an Eagle Scout, the highest possible in Boy Scouts. This was a big task for me. I had to do a lot of extra community service, earn merit badges, and set a good example for the other kids. At sixteen, when all the other boys got their Eagle, I was still a long way from getting mine. I decided to wait it out and see if my parents wouldn't cave in and tell me to just go ahead and get my license. But they were adamant and their minds couldn't be changed. By the time I turned seventeen, I could see that they were dead serious about me earning my Eagle. All of my friends had their licenses, and for transportation I always had to bum a ride off them.

But as I was slowly approaching my eighteenth birthday, the cut-off age for getting an Eagle, I started to hustle. I definitely wanted a license by my senior year.

I worked hard and did my big Eagle project, and it seemed like I had made it just in time. But the hardest part of getting the Eagle is not necessarily earning the badges and doing the projects, it's passing the Eagle Board of Review.
It was a panel of four or more Scout leaders, and you had to stand before them to be interviewed. They wanted to know why you thought you deserved

to be awarded the highest rank in Boy Scouts. I thought I had secured my badge by completing my Eagle Project, but that was far from the case. While the leaders interviewed me, they brought up all the bad things I'd ever done as a Scout, and grilled me with questions. It felt like an interrogation more than an interview. Why did I do all those things? They asked why I hadn't been able to set a good example of Boy Scout virtues. I told them I didn't know. I had no answers for my scouting behavior. It just was what it was. I made no excuses, but neither did I accept responsibility.

After they were done asking me their series of questions, the reviewers asked me wait outside in the hall while they discussed my worthiness to obtain the Eagle. After waiting for a long time on pins and needles, I started to get worried about what might happen. They had the power to deny me my Eagle Scout ranking, and that meant I wouldn't be getting my driver's license. If I didn't have my license, I wouldn't be cool for my entire senior year. As I entered the room, they all looked at me with somber faces. I knew right away something was wrong. They informed me that I hadn't set a good enough example for scouting, and they were not passing me through the Eagle Board of Review. But they did decide to postpone their final decision, which bought me a few weeks. At the end of that time, I could come back and give them a more convincing reason as to why I should be an Eagle Scout. Basically they wanted me to beg them for it. I despised the fact that they had the power and authority to stop me from getting my license. But I thanked them for the chance to return and argue my case.

That was a long couple of weeks, and embarrassing for my Mom and Dad. They were both very big supporters of scouting, especially since my two older brothers were certified Eagle Scouts. I couldn't believe I'd been denied.

For all my years of scouting, this was what it had come down to. I thought for the next couple weeks about how scouting had affected me and how it had played a positive role in my life. When I went back to stand before the Review, I thanked them again for the opportunity, and the leniency they displayed in giving me a second chance. I then turned on my charm and told them how much scouting had helped me grow. I apologized for all my erratic behavior and told them that I felt sad about not having applied myself in a better manner. I told them I worked hard for my Eagle Scout, and had set a good example for my troop on the Eagle Project. I said I had evolved as a Scout, and that holding me accountable for my past behavior would be short-sighted. I had grown a lot in the past year, and Scouts was all about personal growth and turning into a man. I made them feel comfortable about letting me pass. I had convinced them that I would now take scouting seriously, and pass on the spirit of personal growth to others.

They passed me and I was ecstatic! I felt like I had started to evolve into a man, and now had to live up to the responsibility of being an Eagle. I learned the hard way, but the Eagle is a bird who is a leader and never flies in a flock. They are the true noble birds that soar above all others. I was now considered one of them. I no longer wanted to be considered a pigeon. I was an Eagle! And even to this day, I try to live up to the promise I made, that I would be an example of what an Eagle does. I take pride in the fact that I did earn my badge, working hard and atoning for my past actions. I'm grateful that they gave me a second chance to prove myself.

Here is an incident in which I almost got shot.

In high school, I would sometimes affiliate myself with other fighters. They had told me one Friday at school that that night they were going to fight another crew from another school. The fight was to take place at this club off the boulevard we used to cruise our cars on. That night we all met in the parking lot. There was a lot of people hanging out. Our crew was waiting until the other school's crew showed up. In the meantime, we were acting crazy and loud. We saw another crew gathering, a gang who didn't like our high school. They started giving us dirty looks, then came up to us yelling and threatening. It turned into a huge brawl. Everyone was swinging.

Others were joining them and we had to back up, eventually retreating. I ran across the street to wait the rumble out, but there were a bunch of people following me. The fight had spilled out into the street by now. People were running everywhere. All of a sudden I heard gun shots, and fear started to pump through my veins. My heart was beating out of my chest, and I was trying not to get caught up in the crossfire. Everyone was running and scrambling around like crazy when another gunshot went off. The bullet from that gunshot hit the garbage dumpster right behind me. I thought I was going to be killed. I just ran in a panic down the street as fast as I could when I saw my friend drive by in his truck yelling, "Derek get in!" I didn't even hesitate, jumping into the back of the truck and getting face down as we went tearing down the highway.

I was definitely a rebellious kid. I didn't rebel by doing drugs or drinking alcohol. I never got into experimenting with drugs, and in fact I've never tried them. I don't know what it's like to be high, at least not any higher than my crazy personality already made me feel. In school, I would never apply myself. I always preferred to be the class clown or the fighter.
I was never interested in getting good grades, nor

was I into letting authority figures tell me what to do. I was bored a lot. I was a musician and yet I got straight D's in symphonic band class. Man, if my band teacher could only see me now. I have accomplished a lot musically. I just believe that the classroom environment was not well-suited to my brand of self-expression.

I almost didn't graduate high school, due to a particular incident. It was the spring semester, and as usual I was just doing my own thing. I was eighteen most of my senior year, and technically an adult. This meant I could write my own notes to get out of class. I'd normally go to the beach and surf. This was fun, but I don't recommend it—kids, stay in school! One day I was hanging out in English class and, as usual, making rude comments just to get a few laughs. My teacher said to me, "You shouldn't talk like that. You're a Christian and go to those early morning Bible studies." I told her I could do whatever I wanted. She was actually a very nice woman, but because of my immaturity I had no respect for her. I was not afraid to tell her off in front of the whole class.

I verbally exploded on her, like I was the one in charge of class. I called her some very profanity-laced names. I'll just let you imagine what they were. She told me to get out of the class, but I refused, so she called the assistant principal to come and get me. I took my bag and got out of there before the assistant principal came. I ran. I was gone. Later that day, I showed up at the assistant principal's office and sat down to tell her I'd been kicked out of the class. She already knew, of course, and informed me that the teacher never wanted me back in her class again, on account of my language and disrespect. They decided they were going to expel me from school.

I had to call my Mom from the assistant principal's office and tell her what happened. I let her know that I was no longer allowed to be in school. I went home, very embarrassed and very much in trouble. My parents got involved and were able to save me from being completely expelled. I ended up only expelled from English class, and I now had to take English in the assistant principal's waiting room every day. If I didn't show up and do my work I'd be expelled completely.

This happened a couple months prior to graduation, and I'd heard from my counselor that I wasn't on track to graduate. This was unbelievable to me. I couldn't fathom that I was going to flunk high school. She said the only way to make sure I graduated was to bring my grades up within a month. Despite the warning, I didn't try any harder. Then when all of my friends were ordering their special graduation announcement cards; ordering their caps, gowns, and tassels; and planning their graduation parties, I was totally bummed and felt like a failure. I didn't even bring the order sheet home to my parent's because I knew I wasn't going to be getting my diploma. It was embarrassing having to tell my friends that I wouldn't be walking the graduation stage with them. I was ashamed. I remembered how I'd been kicked out of my kindergarten class, and now here I was basically getting kicked out of high school. I decided at that point, at the eleventh hour, to get serious and apply myself. If I could at least get some passing grades I could walk the stage with my classmates.

Over the next month I was doing all of my homework and working hard, but I didn't know for sure if this effort would be enough to earn the required grades. I worked and worked without having any idea of what the end result might be.

Then about a week before graduation, my counselor called me into her office and told me I would be able to graduate. I had done what was barely sufficient to make it. I was ecstatic and overjoyed. I could not believe it! This was the best news I'd heard in a long time. I told all of my friends and family, and they were totally excited. The next mission was to get a tassel, cap and gown. So I borrowed my friend's extra tassel, which he had hanging from his car mirror. I borrowed my foster brother's cap and gown, which he still had from his graduation a couple of years before mine. It was torn up from partying the day of his graduation. Adding to its shabbiness was the fact that my brother was about five foot, ten inches, but I was six foot, five inches. The gown was way too short and the cap barely fit my big head. But it worked. I walked that stage with profound gratitude and a happy sense of accomplishment. I had managed to graduate with a 1.83 GPA. Talk about cutting it close.

I could go on and on about the many times I got into trouble for yelling profanities at my parents or getting into fights with teachers, church leaders, and other adults. But that would be a book in itself. All that's left to say is that I am eternally grateful to my foster Mom and Dad for never giving up hope on me. They never changed the locks on the front door or told the social worker to take me away. They serve as great examples of love and patience, enduring as they did the hard times which inevitably come when raising a messed up little kid. They didn't have to keep me. I wasn't adopted, so they could have given up on me at any time. But instead they chose to never give up on me, even when I gave them hell. They always shot back with a love that came from deep within their hearts, proving that love has the power to overcome the negative in any situation. Thank you so much Mom and Dad!

EVERYTHING IS A CHOICE

Making good choices is the single most important element of the critical thinking process. Good choices will aid you in living the life you want to lead, and determine whether the sum character of that life is positive or negative. The wisdom of others who have gone through life before us tells us how crucial making the right choices is to living the good life. Wherever you happen to be in life, there is somebody out there who has already walked the same road. The situations of your life are not original. If you want to understand how life operates, ask someone older than you. Chances are they have been where you are, or know how to avoid the pitfalls you are at risk of falling into. The older they are, the wiser they should be.

A lot of people make choices based on logic alone. I don't rely on logic only. Logic, for example, tells you that if you put your hand in a fire, it will get burned. A lot of my decision-making is based on intuition. Some people call it gut or heart, but whatever it is, it is within you, a part of yourself. I call it your soul's consciousness. Whether marrying my wife at a young age or opening a business, all my most important decisions have been made by intuition rather than logic. Logic is overly cautious, and would have told me to wait until I had a job to marry my wife, so that I could better support her while she was in school. And logic would have also told me that there is far too much risk in starting your own company. Logic may be right for a lot of other people, but it wasn't always right for me. I went with my gut and it paid off great!

Don't let negativity get stuck in your mind, just let it blow away. No one knows you the way you do. Don't let anyone criticize and demean your inner spirit!

You cannot please everyone, but you can please yourself. If you take care of yourself first and become happy, this happiness will shine through. People will notice and wonder what makes you such a happy and special person. It will seem abnormal, since there are so many unhappy people walking the planet. We are either going forwards or backwards. We cannot stay still. We are always in motion. Every action is based on a choice, and the sum of these choices determines our life. It is your choice, simple as that.

I completely trust myself. I know that my instincts, my inner self, will not lead me in the wrong direction. It is my compass. We are all wired with "God-

Given Common Sense." We have an inner self we consult with to determine whether we should or should not do something. There is an internal debate that goes on within yourself when making a decision, and this debate is how you justify your actions.

Of course, sometimes we use this internal debate to justify destructive actions. There is a strong instinct for self-destruction at times, what Freud called the "death-wish." I believe I had a death-wish for a long time. I was constantly in fights and pushing the boundaries set by adults. I had no fear! I have never let fear hold me back from doing or saying what I want. But the trick is to be fearless in constructive ways.

Decisions based on fear can hurt others in ways we don't always anticipate. My mother and stepfather were fearful of me, and justified giving up and getting rid of me by saying they couldn't control me. When I was younger I believed their motives were purely selfish. Now, being older and wiser, I consider my mother's actions in a somewhat different light. I believe she knew she could not provide the right kind of life for me, considering all the problems I had. Yes, she said horrible things about me as a kid, but looking back, I understand that she did the right thing. Growing up, though, I despised her for giving up her "blood" son. I realize my stepfather was largely responsible for the decision to get rid of me, but ultimately, if my mother had stood up to him and said, "This is my son! I will not get rid of him!", I would have had a lot more respect for her in my youth.

U-R.O.C.K
FINDING THE LEADER WITHIN

This chapter is all about choice. It's about understanding that you have the power to create or change
your destiny. One of the most important lessons I
have learned in life is not to let my past infect my
future. I apply this lesson every day. Think about
some time in your life, a time that has been really
tough to overcome. Or think about some troubling
event you keep dwelling on. What happens while
you're dwelling on the past is that you become so
obsessively fixated on a particular incident that it
hinders you from moving forward with your life.
You must have the ability to let things go. This isn't
always easy, I understand. I have let the pain of my
past infect my future at times, and it has certainly
held me back. I've been lost, not knowing what
direction to take in my life. There have been times
when all I could think was, "Why me?" But you
must understand that this mentality, this fixation on
the negative, will almost certainly ensure that your
future will be filled with more of the same.

Your parent's mistakes, or your own mistakes for
that matter, don't have to define the person you are.
You never have to stop living a rewarding life!

Remember, your best days are still ahead of you! And if your past has been troubled, this is the case to an even greater degree. Your teenage years represent just a small fraction of what the rest of your life will offer. But remember, though there is always time to make changes in your life, the choices you make in your teenage years will set the course for your life in the future. Teens today face countless challenges. Sometimes it seems like there are more opportunities for trouble than positive achievement. Teens may get addicted to drugs, alcohol, join a gang, kill, steal, go to jail or become involved in a teenage pregnancy. These problems will definitely follow you into adulthood. Save yourself the trouble of dealing with these problems later, and don't become involved with them as a young person. Instead of falling behind, forge ahead!

Everyone suffers, but what we do with that suffering makes all the difference. How will we use our pain to shape and determine our future? Will we torture ourselves just for the sake of it, or will we learn from our suffering, using it as a tool to enrich our future? When you change the way you think about your pain, your life will change in dramatic and inspiring ways. I realized as a young man that I didn't have to feel guilty and blame myself any longer for the pain my mother, father, and other people caused me. I had to take responsibility for my own life and not let any other person control my heart and mind. It was time for me to take leadership over my own life. I needed to unload this twenty-thousand-pound backpack of emotional distress, anger, rage, and sense of being valueless. No longer was I going to suffer at the hands of others' past mistakes, or even my own. I realized that I wanted to be a victor in life and no longer a victim. I wanted to ROCK!

There is a simple formula that I have used to bring more meaning into my life. It is a program I teach when I do seminars. It is called I-R.O.C.K. It is an acronym for how I live my life, as well as how I inspire others to live theirs.

I is for Integrity
R is for Responsibility
O is for Opportunity
C is for Choice
K is for Knowledge

Integrity is the most important quality. Integrity can be measured by how well you live up to your own principles and values. Often we fail to meet our own standards and expectations, but if we gave it our best shot, our integrity remains intact. That part of yourself, this person who holds you accountable to a higher standard, is the person who assesses your integrity. This is who you are when the lights go out and you are alone with your own conscience. You cannot hide from yourself. Integrity is about being honest in your dealings with both others and yourself. Integrity concerns what people think about you when you are not around – your reputation. It's about how people perceive you, and what message you are sending to others about your character. This is also how you perceive yourself. Do you hold yourself up with dignity? Do you have respect for yourself and others? Having integrity is about sending a message to your family, friends and coworkers – now and in the future - that you are truthful and reliable. What you expect from others you should also expect from yourself.

"The ideas that have lighted my way have been kindness, beauty and truth."- Albert Einstein

Responsibility is what determines whether your life is more about being a victim or more about being a victor. Taking responsibility for your words, thoughts, actions and emotions literally changes the quality of your life. This is your life, and you have to take responsibility for it. This means being accountable for your actions and words. I believe a big part of taking responsibility is releasing the poison in your heart. The only way to do that is to forgive. Forgiving others who have done you wrong, and forgiving yourself, are both crucial to achieving a happy life. I know from experience. I was poisoning my life by not letting go of earlier pain.

I once heard this saying: "Do you know what the most flammable piece of wood is? The chip on your shoulder." As a teenager, I used to walk through life with a giant chip on my shoulder. I was mad at everyone who I felt was against me. And if you weren't for me, you were against me. I was totally disrespectful to other people and to anybody who was an authority. Part of my problem was that I was not taking complete responsibility for my direction in life. I was used to blaming others for my situation and the way I was. I blamed my Mom for giving me up and keeping my brother and sister. I blamed my Dad for not even caring about his own son. I blamed my foster parents because at times I felt like they prohibited me from going home to my biological mother, even thought that wasn't a rational or logical thought.

I have had to learn and relearn that you can't believe everything you think. Every thought that comes into your mind must be filtered. You have to ask yourself whether a thought contributes positively or negatively to your life. Is it a negative, toxic voice that wants to attach its ugly self to your brain, and eventually take over your heart and soul? I often believed that everyone was out to hurt me, and it was this that made me the way I was. But blaming others will only stop you from really enjoying this life. You start to think that everyone is out to get you in some way, when in reality all that is hurting you is your own attitude. Make a commitment right now. Tell yourself that you are going to take responsibility for your life. Tell yourself that you will not lay blame on anybody else, or play the role of the pitiful victim. You are going to get back up, dust yourself off, and be stronger and wiser. This is your life! If you don't take responsibility for it, who will? Start today, so you don't have any regrets for wasted yesterdays.

"You cannot escape the responsibility of tomorrow by evading it today." - Abraham Lincoln

Opportunity is your chance to have exactly what you want in life. Opportunity may seem like a hidden thing, or something vague. But the good thing about opportunity is that it's always right there in front of you, ready for you to reach out and grab it! And once you get hold if it, it will change your life. A lot of people don't go out and take advantage of this fact - the nearness of opportunity. They wait for the opportunity to come to them. In reality, 99% of the time you have to go out and look for it. Once you find it, don't be afraid to go for it! I believe the reason people don't look for the opportunities that could make their life better is fear. Fear of the unknown, fear of failure, the fear of what people will think of them. I say...WHO CARES! This is your life and you better make the most of it.

This is the true meaning of my sayings, Never Give Up and Never Limit Your Life. You have to trust yourself! You must know and believe that you have to explore every opportunity that may contribute to the fulfillment of your dreams, to your job, to your schooling, and everything else in life. There have been many, many people who did something great with their life simply because they had the courage to take a chance, a risk. By risking much, we are often led to opportunities we may never have imagined, or even dreamed of, had we been more timid. I believe success comes when you try to go for as many opportunities as you can. Do this, and you continually push yourself forward in life. There is nothing wrong with failure. Every person who has done something great has met with failure. If you don't try, you will eventually collect so many regrets over wasted yesterdays that you won't have the happy and fulfilling life you might have had – the happy life that you deserve! So go for it, take a chance, and ROCK ON!

"Chance never helps those who do not help themselves." – Sophocles

<u>Choice</u> is probably the biggest factor in whether you are going to live a happy and fulfilling life or a miserable and pitiful life. Everything in life revolves around a choice. It doesn't matter who you are; you could be the wealthiest or the poorest person on Earth. It doesn't matter where you live; you could live in Lithuania or Tasmania or Kentucky. Your age doesn't matter, you can be young or old. Who we are as individuals is just the sum of the choices we've made. Our first and most important choice concerns our attitude toward life - how do we react to the world at large? Be grateful for this time we've been given on Earth, and everything else will fall into place. Even the challenges can bring great happiness, if we react positively to life. Problems can be temporary if we don't attach ourselves to them and make it a part of our identity.

Think about it: everything in your life is a choice. Even when you don't make a choice, you are really choosing to not choose! This may seem silly, but it is actually a very profound and important idea. If we are always making a choice, even when choosing not to choose, why not instead be an active chooser? Your choices determine your character – wouldn't you prefer to be self-determined?

Making the right choice is a courageous act, but we often make the wrong ones. But thankfully, with every choice we make in life, whether good or bad, there is something to learn. Certain choices bring punishments, while others bring happiness and peace. I have made choices that have affected other people's happiness. I often chose to be disrespectful, hurt people's feelings, and hurt myself. But instead of choosing to dwell on my past mistakes and be destroyed by guilt, I chose to stop going down the self-destructive path I was on. I also made the choice to rid myself of all my negative feelings, and to look at life from a different perspective. Making the right choice over the wrong has immediate rewards, and you will notice them.

I also chose to learn from my bad choices. For so long, I was making one wrong choice after another, until I realized I was miserable and wanted a happier life. More importantly, it dawned on me that it was all my choice. I had the power to change direction. As soon as I figured out that little secret, my ability to make smarter choices became more conscious and self-directed. I grew wiser, and began to really contemplate my actions and reasons for them. I realized that up to then I'd made decisions based on a reactionary relationship to life. Life would come at me, and I would respond. How much better to push back on the world than have it pushing against you! Once decisions become a matter of conscious choice, and not a matter of simply reacting to outside forces, it totally opens up the field of options. You realize that you have tons of choices that will help you better your life. You may have felt trapped because the world was pressing in on you – but there are endless opportunities once you realize you are free to direct your own will.

Now I desire to make only the right moves. To make the choices that will better my life, instead of help destroy it. As a teenager, you are in a very difficult position. Every day you are faced with many choices to make, and they come at you from all sides. There are people pushing drugs your way, cigarettes, alcohol, gangs and sex. There are people pushing you to do what it takes to try and be popular, or to have certain attitudes that they think are cool. You have pressure to get good grades from one quarter, and bad grades from another. You may have a boyfriend or girlfriend who parents aren't going to approve of. People may think you spend too much time on the phone, the internet, and texting. You may have pressure to respect or disrespect your parents, tell the truth or tell lies. All these things add up to an immense amount of pressure, and sometimes your life literally hangs in the balance.

Making the wrong choice could result in major consequences, punishment, or death. So be wise when making your choices. Adolescence is the practice ground for decision-making. It's there so that when you become an adult, living on your own, you will have gotten a majority of the learning out of the way and will know how to spot the difference between a good choice and a bad one. Then you can focus on new choices that are going to improve your life financially, socially, spiritually, and physically. And then maybe someday, you can have a family of your own, and set a great example for them. So go out there and choose the right!

"You must give up the way it is... to have it the way you want it, it's a choice." -Unknown

Knowledge is the key. Knowledge gives you more options in life. The more you learn, the more you will grow. If I could push you in any direction, I would say: GO TO COLLEGE! Looking back, I wish I had gone to college - but I took a different road. If I had gone to college, I know that I would have been smarter in business, which has been a big part of my life. I had to learn some hard lessons. I learned them, but I wouldn't want others to have to go through the things I did. I suffered a great deal financially as an adult in learning the ins and outs of business practices. A question I often ask myself is, "What if I had gone to school for business?" I would have had much more information on what it means to be in business, and I could have learned from others who had already gone through what I ended up going through.

Always seek advice when you make big decisions. One of my friends passed on some great advice to me, saying "Derek, when you want make a big decision, check with three of your smartest friends." Always make sure you have friends who are smarter than you. These are the people who will help you rise to their level. In high school I didn't hang out with the academic scholars; I mainly hung out with the academically challenged! Now I try to have friends who are smarter than me in areas where I am lacking knowledge. And I hope that I am a useful friend in areas where I am smarter than they are. Friendships should be a healthy balance.

Knowledge is so important to helping catapult dreams into reality. But I also believe that knowledge should go hand-in-hand with imagination. Knowledge is at times a little limited, whereas imagination is completely unlimited. But knowledge will help guide your imagination; controlling and containing it in such a way that it leads to something tangible you can give the world.

Imagine if I became what I've always dreamed about - let's say, for example, I was a professional songwriter. Well, I wouldn't be a very good songwriter if I didn't learn about different types of music, notes, syncopation, tone, melody, timing, rests, and other aspects of music theory. If I didn't know any of that, I would probably end up writing songs that no one would want to hear. Suppose you wanted to be a doctor. You would have to go to school for many years, and then do your residency – basically, learning on the job and applying what you were taught in school. The more you exercise your intelligence and expand your knowledge, the more information you have to make the educated decisions that will impact your life.

So do not be afraid to ask questions! How else are you going to learn and process stuff? Ask away and be curious! In life, everything you do or don't do gets processed in your brain. Your brain labels and stores it. Make sure you are taking in as much information as you can about different cultures, art, music, travel, education, religions, political views, foods, etc.... The more information you have, the greater your understanding will be. If we had more people interested in gathering good information, we would have a lot less ignorance about each other and our differences. We can learn from others all about the different ways of approaching the world. Then, we can choose which bits we want to apply in our own life. Knowledge is power - now go get you some!

So there you have it. When you look in the mirror and are tempted to pick yourself apart because there is something about yourself you don't like, I want you to say out loud "I ROCK!" Give yourself a little love. Look into your own eyes and say it again: "I ROCK!" After saying it, you can't help but feel a little smile creeping onto your face. You know that you have a lot to offer this world, and that you can change the way you feel about yourself. In fact, I want you to say some other things to yourself while you look in the mirror. " I Like Myself! I Am Living This Life Now! I Am Grateful For what I Have, and I Respect Myself Cuz I ROCK!"

Let me end on this note. You have all that it takes to

claim victory in your life. You have the looks, the talent, the attitude, the desire and the power to create the life you have always imagined. Now if you haven't imagined what kind of life you want as an adult, you better start thinking about it. It is better to be prepared than to be scared. Life is about learning and growing every day. Follow your dreams and follow your heart, because your life is going to follow after your thoughts. Today is the day you decide that U ROCK!

"He who asks a question is a fool for a minute; he who does not remains a fool forever."
– Chinese Proverb

I want to point out some things I have learned from taking leadership. I have learned that there are two different kinds of leaders. One who leads for the good, and one who leads for the bad. The worst kind of leaders this world has seen have been those who lead through anger and intimidation. In order for you to be an effective leader, you must first lead yourself. You have to first be a worthy example, so that others will want to follow you. You have to show that you have the skills to lead yourself before you can lead others.

I have come up with an acronym for the word LEADER. I consider this type of leader to possess the absolute worst traits possible, the traits that make a bad leader. Usually acronyms are positive sugges-tions and ideas. But with a negative acronym, you can see the difference between a good leader and a bad one.

L - Lazy - leader doesn't do the work or put in the time.
E - Egotistic - leader thinks they are better than everyone else.
A - Angry – leader shows violent and disrespectful behavior.
D - Dishonest – leader doesn't have integrity or tell the truth
E - Eternally complaining or manipulating others
R - Removes themselves from responsibility when things get tough.

Now here are the qualities of a great leader!

L - Learns how to turn their weaknesses into their strengths
E - Ethical - Encourages others to succeed - Enthusiastic
A - Appreciates others - Action-Taker - great Attitude - Acknowledges others
D - Determined - never gives up without a fight
E - Example to follow- Empathetic, understands oth-ers
R - Responsible - Reliable - Ready to act with strength and courage

So which leadership qualities would you rather possess? As for myself, I choose the second set. These are great traits to take on and develop. Remember, leadership begins with leadership over yourself. Act towards yourself the way you would towards the people you might lead. I know that if you take on these traits, your life will be happier, and people will want to be around you. People naturally gravitate towards great leaders. You'll radiate an exciting energy, and you'll train yourself to exhibit the self-discipline and control necessary to march bravely through the rough patches in life. A great leader also remains calm in times of adversity.

You have within you so much potential! Every one of us has the potential to become a great leader. It is your choice. If you follow the I-R.O.C.K. principals, you will find it much easier to conduct your life in a productive and influential way. A great leader can turn hopelessness into the power of hope by encouraging others. Once you help others find hope, they will in turn share it with others. It becomes a ripple effect, continually moving forward, until many people feel the positive vibe. I have had the great opportunity to lead others to success. As a leader, I have been tested by life's many hardships. These trials and hard times allowed me opportunities to shine, thrive, and become a stronger person. I chose to learn from the hard times. You too have the ability to be a courageous, strong, successful, and great leader! You can achieve your wildest dreams. Believe me, you have what it takes!

IDENTIFY YOUR IDENTITY

As a teenager, my identity must have been one of the toughest things to find. Think about this for a second - do you know who you are? Besides just being a body going through life, surviving, really think about it for a minute. When nobody else is around, and you look at yourself in the mirror, do you really know who it is looking back at you? What makes you unique? Your parents, teachers, friends and everybody else might have formed an identity for you, or given you a label - but is it really accurate? When all the noise in your head is gone, who are you? Or even better, WHO DO YOU WANT TO BE?

In high school, my identity was a fighter, a skater, a rapper, and a class clown. But I totally wished that my identity was a lady's man, a massive chick-magnet! Even though I had girlfriends, I wanted more, more, more! I wanted the world to love me. I yearned for love and affection. If I wasn't getting any, I would find another way to get some. Generally, that meant doing a bunch of bad stuff and goofing off.

I know now that how I acted out was the wrong way to get attention. Instead, I could have first given love, and been the example of what I needed back. I didn't do that. I was into keeping my walls up, making everyone else prove their loyalty to me before I would let them in. Sometimes you just have to let the walls you've built around yourself fall down. Let people in, and let them take a look around to see if they like what they see! If they don't, no biggie, just move on. Someone will eventually like what they see. In the meantime, you are evolving and forcing yourself to grow every time you get to know someone and let them get to know you.

I want you to know right now, that whatever identity you've been labeled with doesn't have to be correct. Even if you have accepted other people's labels, or have given yourself a negative one, it is now time to change it. I am a firm believer in changing your identity status and making your heart tell your body what you want to be. So what if you have made mistakes and your identity is all rolled up and confused with those mistakes? Change is always good if they are positive changes.

For example, let's say you've used drugs and alcohol. Your friends and family might say that you're a drug user or an addict, but I am here to tell you that it doesn't matter if you've made some poor choices! Your past mistakes don't have to define who you are now, or who you'll be tomorrow. You are not your past mistakes. Nor, for that matter, are you your parent's mistakes. You are not a worthless person with no value! You are not a loser! You are special. When you look in the mirror, do you pick yourself apart? Point out all the flaws, zits, and scars? Do you focus on how big your nose is, or how big your ears are? Maybe you don't like the color of your eyes or your hair. This could be a huge problem! We all have things about ourselves we'd like to change. But picking yourself apart brings negative energy into your heart and mind. Soon, you start to identify with the negative, with what you don't like about yourself.

Imagine if you looked in the mirror and said to yourself, "You know what? I ROCK! I am beautiful and I like myself and what I look like." If you were to totally focus on the things that you like about yourself, like your looks, talents, generosity, niceness, selflessness and willing to help others, you attract even greater and more positive things to yourself. Positivity breeds positive outcomes, and negativity breeds the negative. How can you ever expect to live a positive life when you're always thinking negatively about yourself? You cannot speak and think negatively and attract positivity.

It all starts with what is inside your heart. Make your identity work in tune with your behavior. It is now time to see yourself in a more positive manner, one that correlates more closely with the vision of yourself that you hold in your heart. Changing your identity on the fly all the time doesn't really do anything. You need something deeper and more lasting. You need to change your beliefs before you change your outward appearance.

Let's say that one day you are a rocker, then the next day you're a rapper, and the next you're a cowboy, but secretly you've always been a Mozart concerto admirer. You are leading a double-life to fit in with others. My advice is to be true to yourself and your own passions. It's alright to try new things, but if you want to make new things a part of your identity, do it in a way that you still remain true to yourself. That means when the lights go out and it's just You, having a conversation with You, You aren't going to try and lie to yourself right? You may be able to fool the world, but in the end you can't fool yourself.

I have come to realize that life is most rewarding when you're moving forward instead of backwards. You may have taken on some of these identities and felt like you had to live with them, but you don't. In a second, you can change your outlook on life and change who you are. The thing is, you have to make a change first in your heart and soul, then don't forget to tell your face about it, so that it mirrors the attitude of your heart.

I have to be honest. I used to have a secret identity. Instead of being "Super Man", I was "Pain Man". My defensive walls were always up, and nobody could see that I was dying inside - dying emotionally. I was wounded and in pain throughout high school. I would mask it on the outside with the identity I created. Everyone saw me as a clown and fighter. I would literally torture my soul by not sharing my pain with anyone else. I kept it bottled up until I discovered that I had a talent for rap. So in high school I started to rap. My name was Diamond, because a diamond is unbreakable and solid like a rock. I could beat-box, I could spit the lyrics and flow. I was the D-I-A-M-O-N-D! I loved it. I could express myself through music and challenge others to rap battles. Growing up in the San Francisco Bay Area, I found many opportunities to express myself in competitions against others. I would sometimes win and sometimes lose, but ultimately I had found a creative outlet to slowly release my pain. This turned out to be just the beginning stage of releasing my soul into the world.

Diamond is just one of the identities that has followed me around in my life. It is a true, authentic part of me, and I love sharing it with the crowds. Diamond is good for breaking stereotypes and shattering preconceptions about how I am supposed to be. It is a big surprise when Diamond comes out of the box, and he teaches people that you can't just judge a book by its cover. You never know how other people might surprise you. More importantly, you never know how you might surprise yourself.

MY MUSIC IS MY THERAPY

Music is simply amazing. Next to my family, my music is the most important thing in my life. I am not talking about going to concerts or turning on the radio. I mean creating music from the wellspring of the soul. My testimony of life, my faith and my beliefs are expressed through the musical melodies circulating around my soul. My sadness, anger and happiness are turned into a song, where they become almost as precious to me as the children I have created. I can't tell you which song is my favorite. It's like telling you which of my kids is my favorite. It is impossible to say, but I can tell you that creation is in tune with the music of your heart. Music can change the mood you're in. You can go from sadness and anger to an energetic happiness. Finding just the right sound can bring tears to your eyes. When composed with passion, music is nothing less than miraculous. It can literally heal the emotionally wounded.

I will always be indebted to my foster father for passing the miracle of music on to me. I started learning music when I was about eight years old. My foster father played piano and would teach me the basics of music theory and accompany me on duets. He also laid the foundation for me never giving up. He never let me quit when it became hard to learn. Sometimes

I couldn't stand playing the clarinet. But he would make me memorize pages of music for performances. I didn't like it much then, but I eventually got very good at memorizing pieces and playing them well, which helped me blossom into a competent musician, giving me confidence and greatly increasing my self-esteem.

My foster father was committed to teaching me the love of music, and would work with me twice a day in an effort to help me improve. He put me in private lessons for years and made sure that I was enrolled in the school band. I played the clarinet for years. I got very good at that clarinet and won some major competitions at the university level when I was only twelve years old. I wasn't born with the ability to play music. It was a lot of hard, agonizing work. That licorice stick (clarinet) became my buddy and we became one. I soon became recognized as an accomplished clarinet player. The fact that people liked what I was doing and the person I was becoming helped bolster my sense of self-worth. I am indebted to my foster father for never giving up on me, and passing his talent down. Now I can pass the love of music on to my own children.

Music has dramatically changed my life. It has given me the ability to express feelings which otherwise would have remained locked in my soul. Music was the key to the cell that I was trapped in. Music is literally like another language. Playing music is fun, but creating music can change your life. The feeling that overcomes you when you're inspired to create and let your soul breathe free can leave you stunned. It is true inspiration. When you attain the musical ability that allows you to express your deepest emotions, you can sit with a guitar in your hand and sing about what you are feeling at any given moment. It is beautiful how the words just flow out.

When I was eight years old, I decided right then and there that someday I was going to be a rock star, and everyone would like me and love my music. Well, I never became a rock star in the world's eyes, but I am a rock star to my own children. They absolutely love that I play music to them. I also learned that not everyone is going to like my music and that you can't go through life always looking for other people's approval and acceptance. I admit that's a tough thing to accept sometimes, because everyone wants to be liked, and I'm no different in this regard. Being a foster kid makes you feel rejected, and you consider yourself unworthy. Music was the vehicle which allowed me to open up and dream. Dreams can give you hope, and hope was the only thing I needed.

Music has taught me appreciation for the little things. My music gives form to the feelings I have inside. When I am inspired to write, it comes from some deep place in the heart. I have had many opportunities to sing my songs in public performances and see how the music affects others. It is humbling to know that one of my songs can comfort another person, and give them strength to endure a hard time. That is one of the main reasons I like country music.

If you ever want to get real and simple, turn on a country radio station and listen to the words of these songs. They write graciously about simple, everyday situations that people live through. It may be a song about a child stricken with cancer, a son's view of a stepdad, death of a loved one, first love, family bonds, loving America and starting your life all over again. People connect with music. I am not ashamed to have cried numerous times while listening to a song that touched me deeply. In fact, there was a time when on Saturday mornings I would turn on the TV and watch country music videos, and would consistently have a Saturday morning cry. It used to be a joke between my wife and I, when I'd say "Honey, I just had my Saturday morning cry."

Music has helped me to get in tune with other people and come to know their spirits, needs and intentions. It has helped me stay grounded and real. It has allowed me to maintain a connection with my soul and spirit, instead of shunning or hating myself. I like myself and love myself, not in some self-absorbed manner that makes me egotistical or narcissistic, but in a way that allows me to be proud of how far I have come. I like that for most of my life I have gone forwards instead of backwards, and that I try everyday to improve myself in some way.

I have written personally revealing songs since I was seventeen years old. The following song lyrics have been put to music and professionally recorded. I have decided to share them with you so that you may see how I expressed myself during some difficult times.

I wrote "I Wanna Be A Kid" when I was thirty years old. My wife and I had been married for seven years at that point, and decided we wanted to have a child. This was a huge deal and a big step for me. Before we were married we discussed the possibility of not having children.

I was a product of a messed up relationship and therefore had a messed up childhood. I was reluctant to bring any more children into this evil and cruel world. When we decided to have a child, she was pregnant within a month. "Holy cow, that was very quick," I said. I was shocked and grew very scared wondering what kind of father I was going to be. I felt unworthy to take care of a baby angel. I was facing a flood of emotions and bad memories. I could feel the little foster kid inside me beginning to cry. I felt vulnerable. I decided to write a song to my mom, to show her that I can be a winner, and that nobody was going to stop me from soaring in my life. This song has been an inspiration to many. This is my anthem. Its message is that if I can make it in life, then anybody can make it.

I have been questioned about the meaning of the chorus, which says "Bunk to Bombay." It means a bunk bed to somewhere far away. I was tired of bunk beds at the foster homes. I just wanted to escape. If you go to my website www.iwillnevergiveup.com, you can hear this song and watch the music video.

This song has touched so many people. The following email was written by a military psychologist serving in Iraq, describing how her platoon felt about the song:

"Everyone in the platoon, including myself, has never known a mother. There is only one of us who knew their Dad. Everyone in the platoon grew up in foster care and orphanages. Nobody is complaining. Let's just say we all came up through the school of hard knocks. When the platoon heard Derek Clark's song "I Wanna Be a Kid," they all wept tears that were long in coming; very needed and very healing. This song has become our platoon anthem and we listen to it several times a day.

"Recently, another US Marine, Kong, and myself were WIA (Wounded in Action). During the course of getting medical evacuation from a fire-fight, we both had a surreal experience. As Kong and I floated in and out of consciousness, we both had a vision of a huge angel coming toward us, telling us to hang on, and throughout the time this angel was present, we heard Derek singing the words to his song, "I Wanna Be a Kid." The music was so loud it was like we had a $400 Bose head-set clamped on our heads. The pure, pristine sound of Derek singing that song played over and over as we were taken care of by the medics and taken to the combat hospital. The angel kept saying, 'Listen to the song, there is more to come....'

"The platoon and I feel that his words *I wanna fly* symbolizes the freedom found in conquering the past with the help of God and His angels, and flying free to a better future." – Dr. Ariane T. Alexander "Doc"

I WANNA BE A KID

BY DEREK W.CLARK

You want to see me cry, you want to see me die,
You want to look into my eyes
And see the devil's eyes,
You want to see me smile with my battle scars
But if you look into my eyes,
You'll see an Angel's heart,
It was 1975, I was 5,
Momma I was looking at you all surprised
But you were looking at me with fear,
And all along Momma, you didn't want me here.

(Chorus)
I wanna fly, bunk to Bombay,
Here I am in this world today,
I wanna fly, bunk to Bombay
Here I am, I need a home today.
No more Foster Homes and no more Orphanage,
I just wanna be a kid.

So here I am in the struggle of the human race,
But no one wants me, my face, I feel so disgraced,
I'm just an orphan in line, like a lamb to a slaugh-
ter,
I could be a good son, but no one bothers,
Well the good Lord works in mysterious ways,

He opened Heavens gates for only one day,
And the Angels of courage and Love were sent,
There was this one loving Family, that took me in.

(Chorus)
I wanna fly, bunk to Bombay,
Here I am in this world today,
I wanna fly, bunk to Bombay
Here I am, I need a home today.
No more Foster Homes and no more Orphanage,
I just wanna be a kid.

I've got a sad past, everyday a ghost haunts me,
They can't harm me, I've got a family,
I've got a son, a wife, I've got a true life,
It's been given back to me, I'll do it right,
They'll never live the Hell that I have been through,
I can guarantee that, I swear to you,
This is real, this is my life,
If I can fly, you can fly.

(chorus)
I wanna fly, bunk to Bombay,
Here I am in this world today,
I wanna fly, bunk to Bombay
Here I am, I need a home today.
No more Foster Homes and no more Orphanage,
I just wanna be a kid.
Don't leave me alone Mom.

I just wanna be a kid.
Don't leave me alone Mom

"Everything is Nothing" was written at the point in my life when I had achieved financial success. I had become consumed with making money, and recognized that the more hours I worked, the more money I would make. I thought I was happy. But I realized one day that, though I had all the toys and money in the bank, my relationship with my wife and children was suffering. I was not happy. I did not have the balance of family in my life.

I justified long hours at work by telling myself I was providing for my family, but the truth is that my wife and children didn't care how big our house was, what car I drove, or how much more money I could put in the bank. They just wanted their husband and Daddy home. I wanted to love, but I had lost myself. I had everything, but I was alone. This song expresses the guilt I felt as I was trying to get myself back together and remind myself what is really important in life.

It was a hard cycle to break. I felt like I had a disease, and couldn't shake off being addicted to work.

It was hard for me to love, and to think of anyone besides myself. I had lost touch with my soul, spirituality, and family. I was more interested in my image, what people thought about me, and how successful I was than I was with what was REAL. What was "REAL" was that I had a beautiful family at home. I had everything a man could want; a beautiful and supportive wife who continually took care of me, a wonderful child, and all the extra material possessions. I realized I was building an empire of DIRT and nothing more.

Everything comes from dirt, and everything returns to dirt. I couldn't take any of the material possessions with me when I died. There won't be any luggage rack attached to my coffin. How much of your value is based on material and external wealth, rather than internal wealth? I thought, "What would my family remember about me if I was to die? Was I a great husband and a loving father who spent time with his family? Was I putting enough time into what I valued most?" I can honestly say that I now have my priorities straight. Through this storm of adversity, I grew as a human being. I thank my wife and children for their constant support and for never giving up on me.

EVERYTHING IS NOTHING
BY
DEREK W. CLARK

I'd bleed for you, I'd die for you
I'd live the rest of my life, to grow old with you
But the angels don't cry for me
Because I am one of those diseased
And there's no way out from destroying my self
These prison walls are falling on me

(Chorus)
Everything is nothing
I'm feeling all alone
Everything is darkness

Why can't I feel love
You crucified me for what I was
I'd die a real slow death
So you could hear what I'd say in my last breath
And the angels they want to see

All the love that I got in me
I want to give it to you but I don't know how
I want to find what you really want in me

(Chorus)

Everything is nothing
I'm feeling all alone
Everything is fragile
My heart has almost stopped
Everything is darkness
The light is almost gone
Everything is nothing
It's nothing to me

Well life has a way of digging up the past
And these bones shatter like glass
I think I'm crazy or scared of me
Somebody help, I have a disease.

(Chorus)
Everything is nothing
I'm feeling all alone
Everything is fragile
My heart has almost stopped
Everything is darkness
The light is almost gone
Everything is nothing
It's nothing to me

"Goodbye to Goodbyes" was very recently written, just before I started this book. I had just looked at my case file with the county regarding my past as a five year-old kid. I was very sad for two days after seeing how this kid had come into this world. I felt that I finally needed to say goodbye to the past and move on. I didn't want to pass this "history disease" on to my kids. I realized that a part of me enjoyed the pain of my past, and that it might swallow me up and turn me into a person I never wanted to be. I realized that carrying all this weight was holding me down.

I felt like a huge, successful, strong train that was carrying this fifty ton magnet which only allowed me to go forward a little at a time. If I could release this giant magnet, I could go so much faster as a train on the way to its destinations in life. Now I want to be a speeding train. If I allowed my pain to rule my mind, my kids would pick up on it and possibly make my pain theirs. So I took that pain and anguish and finally released it. I had a sad day of acknowledging my past and who I was, and it took a little while to realize that I'm not that person anymore. That was a five year-old kid and I could no longer let that kid have a voice in my head or play a part in my emotions. I decided to look forward and move on.

GOODBYE TO GOODBYES
BY
DEREK W.CLARK

(verse 1)
I've been living here on empty for 36 years,
Seen the life of a lonely man addicted to my fears.
And the hardest part of living is goodbye,
Well I learned this lesson hard when I was 5.

(chorus)
So goodbye to goodbyes,
The hardest part of living is saying goodbye,
I've seen the lonely eyes in my window,
Held the tears of a forgotten son,

I cried for the days when my brother died and
Never said goodbye to mama
When she gave me up, goodbye

(verse 2)
I've been looking back at the picture
Of how I painted my tainted life.
Have I held back love to my wife and children
For the fear of loss in goodbye.
Have I let my fear control me, oh yeah,
Now I've got one life to live,
No more wasting it, no more regrets.

(chorus)
So goodbye to goodbyes,
The hardest part of living is saying goodbye,
I've seen the lonely eyes in my window,
Held the tears of a forgotten son,
I cried for days when my brother died and
Never said goodbye to mama
When she gave me up, goodbye.

(verse 3)
On a lonely road to nowhere
Where your pity leads the way,
Is a man that lost his soul to live,
Where he drinks his life away,
And the memories hard to swallow it all down
When you're a million miles away
Where no one is found.

(chorus)
So goodbye to goodbyes,
The hardest part of living is saying goodbye,
I've seen the lonely eyes in my window,
Held the tears of a forgotten son,
I cried for days when my brother died and
Never said goodbye to mama
When she gave me up, goodbye.

"Goodnight Soldier" was written in the middle of the night, after watching a documentary about the last letter a family received from their son after he was killed in Iraq. I was heartbroken watching it. I was so very touched. My wife and I cried and cried throughout the show. It actually put a human face on the soldier, as opposed to the desensitized descriptions you hear on the news: "Six soldiers were killed today." There is rarely a name or a face to go along with the clip. When we actually saw the face, and got to know in some small way a soldier who was killed, I was powerfully moved. I realized just how extraordinary the sacrifice is that our soldiers make in defending our country. I believe the entire country should come together and show appreciation for our military. They don't get paid much for what they do, and they put everything on the line for us, including their lives.

In America, you have the right to be an anti-war advocate, but you should always support our troops. They are fighting for the right of an anti-supporter to voice his opinion. In many nations, if an anti-supporter voices his opinion, he or she could be put in prison or put to death. Because soldiers fight for you, you are afforded the opportunity to live your life the way you want. This is a beautiful country, and offers us all so much. People die trying to make America their home. We are the greatest country in the world, with opportunity for all, and it didn't get this way by sitting back and doing nothing. Our forefathers had a dream. Some said it was an impossible dream, but they made their dream *your* reality.

The realization of dreams requires sacrifice. What are you willing to sacrifice? This song is a patriotic tribute to the troops, thanking them for their sacrifice, letting them know that I care and respect them for defending our freedom. Freedom isn't a given; we must constantly fight for it so that the next generation can also enjoy it. If the nation one day just up and put an end to all military operations, eventually our freedom would be taken from us. Look around the world, it happens all the time. There are great people in our military, and they are the ones who protect us. They deserve respect. God bless the active service members and the veterans.

GOODNIGHT SOLDIER

BY

DEREK W. CLARK

It's late at night I pray,
For the Lord to guide your way,
I've been watching news every day.
And I don't know you at all,
But look at you standing tall,
As America runs through your veins.

(Chorus)
Good night soldier, good night friend,
'Cause when I'm sleeping here at night,
You're out protecting.
Good night soldier, good night friend,
Please come home,
So I can see you again.

There's a lot of mom and dads who care,
Everyone's a son and daughter out there,
Man, I've cried with love for you all.
I've seen a lot of halo's in the sky,
Lord bless the one's who have died,
Can you tie a yellow ribbon around us all?

(Chorus)
Good night soldier, good night friend,
'Cause when I'm sleeping here at night,
You're out protecting.
Good night soldier, good night friend,
Please come home,
So I can see you again.

WHY ARE PEOPLE DIEING AROUND ME?

I have never liked death or goodbyes. I have lost a foster brother, seven years older than I and as close as any blood brother, and my blood sister, who was ten years older. I have lost foster grandmas and foster grandpas who I considered both great friends and my real grandparents.

I was sixteen years old when I found out that my blood sister was shot and killed by her brother-in-law, in some jealous rage over her filing for a divorce. She was shot in the head. This was on Mother's Day. She left behind two very young children. I had not seen or heard from her since I was five years old. When I was sixteen, I decided to write her a letter and she eventually wrote me back. She wanted to come and visit me. I wrote her back, never to hear from her again. My mother wrote to tell me the sad news of her death. I remember her being so gentle and loving to me. I hadn't seen her since I was put into a foster home. Eleven years later, I was brokenhearted to learn her life had been so brief on this Earth, and that we'd never be able to rekindle our relationship. It is unfortunate that we can never again enjoy the closeness we once shared.

My good friend in high school, and fellow soccer teammate, was killed for no reason. His father took a shotgun and killed him and his little sister while they were sleeping, then turned the gun on himself. I was in shock when the news circulated through school. I remember crying from the realization that life could be taken away at any point. It was unbelievable to think that just the day prior, I was playing soccer and joking around with him, and then the next day he was gone forever. He was a great guy, and I sorely missed him.

One of the most painful deaths was the loss of my foster brother. I was seventeen years old. He had his pilot's license and decided to fly some of his friends out for a weekend of fun. While they were flying over the Sequoia and Kings Canyon National Park, something went wrong and the plane crashed. He and a couple of his friends were killed. There was only one survivor. It was awful. My foster Dad did not allow me to see his body and I am thankful because I would not want to remember my brother in that way. I would rather think of how great a brother he was. He was so accepting of me joining his family.

I remember when I moved into the new foster home, he was in the garage working, and he spoke kindly to me. He taught me how to ride motorcycles and took me camping. He was definitely an important role model in my teenage life. I found out he died when I came home at one in the morning after having been out dancing with some friends. My foster Mom and Dad were crying. I asked them what was wrong and they told me my brother had been killed in a plane crash. I was in state of unbelief. I could not believe my buddy was gone and that I wouldn't see him again in this lifetime. He had just gotten married the year before and had a lovely wife. I remember camping with them and the fun times we had.

After I heard of his death, I locked myself in my room for three days. I cried and cried. He was the only brother I had ever felt close to. I remember getting really mad at God and asking Him why He'd taken away my sister and brother. One of my favorite movies at that time was *The Lost Boys*. It was about a group of young, rebellious vampires, free to do whatever they wanted. There was a new guy wanting to belong to their clique. I felt like that guy, a rebel and wanting to belong. My brother made me feel like I belonged. He made me feel like I was his "real" brother.

There was a song on the soundtrack called "Cry Little Sister," and I played that song over and over for many days. There was one line in particular that always stuck with me: "Come to your brother, thou shall not die....love is with your brother." I felt connected to my brother through this song. I was lonely. I now didn't have an older brother to take me motorcycling or camping, or for just hanging out with at his house. I remember thinking, "Well, now it's my turn to step up and fill the shoes of my older brother, and become the best brother I can be to my little foster brothers and sisters." Those were big shoes to fill, and I never could replace him.

I grew up being a rebel and was completely rebellious throughout my teenage years. But after these deaths I began to recognize that death was a very real thing. People were dying all around me. It took my brother's death to wake me up. I had thought I was invincible. I can't tell you how many times I got in fights, but it was a lot. As a teenager I had a problem with authority. My foster parents and I got in physical altercations when I was younger, and I was always challenging them.

I got into shoving matches with adult church leaders and numerous fights with older teenagers. Even as a little kid, I did not respect or trust authority. I started to really evolve into a good person when my brother died. It really hit home that I was no longer invincible and that I needed to get myself together.

The death of my brother was what really started me on the road to personal change. I finally took ownership of my life and started to make better choices His death taught me that life was immeasurably valuable. I remember going to a three-day therapy seminar on how to move on from your problems and let go of your past. It was helpful, and laid the foundation for understanding myself and others.

So why am I writing all about death in this chapter? Because your life is so very precious. It is irreplaceable. You are the only person who can make it valuable. You can live your life or take your life away. You have the free will to make your life the way you want it to be. You live in the greatest country in the world and have more opportunities than most other people in this world. There are no excuses. We have all heard stories of immigrants who came to this country with nothing, only to become millionaires. All it takes is a dream and hard work to make that dream a reality. But maybe your dream isn't about being a millionaire. Still, whatever you want to be, you have the opportunity to become it in our society.

I have seen how life takes away from the young and the old. Death does not discriminate. You cannot get your life back when you die. Life is not like a video game where you get to restart it and try again. Life is invaluable and cannot be bought back. All the money in the world will not buy your life back or the time that you have wasted. The most delicate and precious thing you have on this Earth is the limited amount of time you have to make the best of yourself and make a positive impact on other people.

Live your life now. People are often so focused on the future they forget to live in the present. I know I am often guilty of that. "Think selfless, not selfish."

There is truth to the saying "Eat, drink, and be merry, for tomorrow you die." I believe it means, live the life you have now at this moment, because you don't know when you are going to lose it. A word of caution, you must be practical and balanced. Live your life like you love it and your positive affirmations will deliver. But you can't fake being positive, your soul knows the truth. You can't lie to yourself, some part of you will detect the lie. Our time here on Earth is limited, do all you can do and be the best you can be.

I came across this quote, I don't know who wrote it, but it poignantly gives you insight as to the value of time.

"To realize the value of ONE YEAR, ask a student who failed a grade.

To realize the value of ONE MONTH, ask a mother who gave birth to a premature baby.

To realize the value of ONE WEEK, ask the editor

of a weekly newspaper.
To realize the value of ONE HOUR, ask the lovers
who are waiting to meet.

To realize the value of ONE MINUTE, ask a person
who missed the train.

To realize the value of ONE SECOND, ask a person who just avoided an accident.

Treasure every moment! Yesterday is history.

Tomorrow is mystery.

Today is a gift. That's why it's called the present!"

-Anonymous

COURAGE TO OVERCOME YOUR FEARS

Don't Let Fear Box Your Life In

What does it mean to be inside a mental mind-box? It means being mentally trapped and closed in. It means not having expanded the independence of your mind. It's letting others tell you who to be and how to act. It's letting others overpower you through manipulation, intimidation, and guilt. It's when fear of failure makes you sweep your ideas, whether brilliant or outlandish, under the rug. It's when every time you want to try something new, your mind builds a wall to barricade you in. It's when you repress and try to hide your desire to dream big.

RISE UP AND STEP OUT OF THE BOX!

There is freedom found in "the box of life" - it's a box without walls. So many people are held back by fear. Fear is nothing more than a thought.

Fear is meant to hold you back. Fear makes us uncomfortable with trying something "outside the box." We seem to place limitations on ourselves, afraid of both the possible and the impossible. Why is this? In a few words, fear of failure, rejection, and of what others might think of us. We need to overcome these mental blocks, busting right through them. As Brendan Francis said, "Many of our fears are tissue-paper thin, and a single courageous step would carry us clear through them." Once you develop the habit of overcoming limiting thoughts, you will be on your way to an action-packed life.

I came from a failing background. But as a child, once I got past the fear of being a failure, the only way I could go was up. I now had a different outlook. No longer was my past going to control me. There was a reason and purpose for my past. When you change the way you look at your life, your life will change. We need to think of these situations as teachers that aid us in improving our character. Throughout my life, I've been stubborn and didn't always take the opportunity to learn lessons from hard knocks, but eventually I did. I wouldn't be writing this book if I never learned, or wasn't able to move forward in a positive direction. Even when we have every advantage in this life, we often choose not to advance in a positive direction.

If we look at ourselves as action-takers and winners, we will no longer settle for a life filled with the "Poor Me Syndrome." When we box ourselves in, allow dreams to fade away, or let the world set limits to what we deserve, we become nothing more than robots with no purpose but to breathe in air and do just enough to get by. Most people want to make a difference in both their lives and the lives of other people, but lack a plan of action. Guess what? The plan will not drop onto your lap and say "Here I am!" You have to make a plan yourself. Life is going to be a crazy maze, but once you have set your purpose and your goal, nobody will ever hold you back again, except you, because ultimately it is your choice how you are going to respond to life.

Never let anyone steal your happiness or try to assassinate your dreams. If they try, brush them off by recognizing that they're not adding to the greatness that is your life. You have to realize that today is your day to start a new life. It is never too late to start all over. It all starts with having a great attitude. I have been known to readjust my attitude during the day when I become too negative. I believe that we weren't meant simply to endure life - we were meant to enjoy it and make the absolute best of it. If we have this attitude, life will deliver something great to us.

YOUR DREAMS ARE NOT IMPOSSIBLE! SEE WHAT YOU BELIEVE! NEVER LIMIT YOURSELF

Do you believe that the impossible is possible? Do you believe that what you can think yourself to be, you can become? Do you believe that dreams are meant to become reality? I am here to tell you to believe beyond your dreams. I try to live my life thinking that I don't want to die before I die. I don't want to live life like a zombie. I want to live my life to the fullest. My spirit imitates my imagination. My creativity comes from my imagination. Whatever your simple mind can dream and create, remember, it can still do so much more. Believe beyond your dreams!

A question anyone might have is, "How do I over-come limiting thoughts?" Well, to answer that question, I am going to go into detail about what I have done in my own life. It all started with a dream. At some point in your life, no doubt, you have had a dream. Maybe it was to be a doctor, an astronaut, professional athlete, race-car driver, artist, President of the United States, or rock star. Even if you don't have a dream right now, you did when you were a child, because every child dreams. Even as adults, we dream. It may be a dream of getting out of an impoverished area, getting a better job, or being rich. Everything is attainable if you focus on what you want and take the action to move towards that goal. Everything is motion, you are either moving forwards or backwards. There is no standing still. When you stand still, you are not moving forward, and if you are not moving forward you are going backwards. Focus on the sky and the stars and not the sewage of this world.

Try to go back in your mind and remember when you were about seven years old, how you felt, how free from the world and responsibilities you were, how you got along with everyone and had love in your heart. Remember how back in the old days there didn't seem to be any worries. Emulate this child you once were, and this child will set your mind free. When your mind is free, you can dream again, taking flight upon the wings you have been given to use. Even if your dream appears ridiculous, be ridiculous in equal measure by believing in it. Where there is laughter and goofiness, there is also the energy to make dreams come true.

As the years pass on, the more serious you become, the more grumpier and stressed out you are. You rarely have time to think about yourself, and opportunities for a good laugh are few and far between.

You become a complainer, believing that life is always unfair. I know, I have been there. Complaining limits you and your dreams. It holds you back from progressing, because you get stuck like a broken record and start throwing pity parties. I love this saying I once heard "When you complain, there you will remain"

What has helped me overcome this grumpy old man's attitude is simply becoming like a child, and just being a goofball. Laugh, laugh and laugh! Think about the innocence of children, and how they are rarely depressed. We as adults teach them by example how to become angry, sad, and disappointed. Children are only about love and being happy. But they pick up on adult behaviors, eventually acting out what they see. So be like an innocent, loving, happy and carefree child, before you learn the destructive patterns this world offers.

Everything starts with energy. Energy creates motion, motion creates action, action creates results, results create achievement, achievement creates self-confidence, and self-confidence creates the mindset that allows you to help others fashion their destiny.

Change the world by changing yourself. Once you are confident about your own ability to achieve, you can help create a world of achievers through your example. People want to be successful and happy. But happiness is rare these days. You can usually spot a happy person because it is so unusual. There are tons of unhappy people who seem uninterested in anything but their own misery. Don't pay them any attention. They will change when they are ready. I heard this saying once: "When the student is ready, the master will appear." It is hard to help someone who doesn't want to help themselves. You can waste a lot of time and energy on people who just don't want to change, because they like the attention they receive when somebody helps them play the victim role.

You absolutely become a product of your environment. Focus on hanging out with people that laugh a lot and are uplifting. I don't care if they are rich or poor, at least they're happy, and you benefit from plugging your mind into happiness, and avoiding negativity and self-conscious suffering. I have heard motivational speakers who say that in order for you to become rich, you must be involved with the rich, act like the rich, smell like the rich, drive a car like the rich, eat like the rich and dress like the rich. I think you can learn from the rich, but most of all be sure you are being true to yourself, and are in search of a meaningful life.

Some of these speakers also say that you shouldn't hang around with poor people, but I am here to tell you that some of the richest people I know are the poorest financially. They are rich in spirit. The accumulation of money does not rule over them, but accumulating the trappings of a meaningful life does. Life is not all about the dollar. Life is about time well spent. Money cannot buy you time. Time is the most valuable thing on earth, you can always make more money but you can't get time back.

I have heard some wonderful stories about how kids with cancer and cancer survivors overcame their heartache with family, music, and laughter. They were all in bad situations, and yet they could still put a smile on their face. These are extraordinary people. Anyone that has been through hell and can still put a genuine smile and on their face is a great person. They laugh in the face of adversity. It is absolutely beautiful!

Don't try to fit in and be somebody you aren't; be true to yourself. Being rich does not mean you are any happier. In fact, it often means more problems. I have had the opportunity to make more money than the average person, and guess what? I don't believe having money made me any happier. When you have money, you get stressed out whenever your savings account starts to dwindle. You freak out from worry over being broke again. Stress overcomes you, because you want to be back on top and have lots of money again. It's a cycle. Being rich is a state of mind. You can be rich in health and family, whereas another person may not have a healthy body or a family, yet has plenty of money. What would you rather have? Money or health? Money or family? Remember, family is the most important thing. I learned that lesson the hard way, but I am glad that I learned it.

I find that a lot of poor people base their wealth on the amount of time they have, instead of on the material possessions they own. They don't need all the fancy cars, houses, and dinnerware. They are more interested in having time to fish, help others in need, and spend time with their children.

See for yourself how many rich fathers spend time with their kids, or how many rich parents have nannies. They are so busy working and making money that they can't be there for their kids. I guarantee that their children are not their first priority. They themselves are their first priority. Remember, it's about being selfless instead of selfish, especially when it comes to helping your children grow up and become amazing adults. All it takes is the time to do it, and then doing it.

Many people who know me know I have a big personality. I like to laugh and joke around. Sure there are times when I have been completely stressed out on one of my big projects. I'm an owner of a company, it happens. And I often allow myself to suffer instead of getting in touch with my soul, which has the power to calm me by letting the voice of reason speak. To regain that lost contact with my soul, I grab my guitar and start writing about my feelings, and in that way pull myself up out of my own hell. At times like these I have often come up with a great song. You might try working out, playing sports, writing, or doing the yard-work.

I love being in the garden. I find peace when I am working with the soil. That soil was created by the God of this world, and sometimes when you're on your knees, weeding the yard, with nothing between you and the soil, an idea pops into your head and you discover a new way to look at your situation.

Another idea is doing something totally "UnYou." In my case, I call it being UnDerek." Do the opposite of what you would normally do. If you don't play sports, get a basketball, go to a park, and try to shoot some hoop. If you are the type that doesn't like to get your hands dirty, then go get your hands dirty and work in the soil. If you hate to write poems, try writing one and express yourself full-heartedly. If you like rock music, listen to classical music or opera. If you like to drink beer and watch TV all the time, try not drinking and go for a hike. The point is to do something opposite of what you would normally do, something outside the walls of a boxed-in life. Don't limit yourself to just those things that make you comfortable. Live a portion of every day being uncomfortable so that you can grow. Get out of your routine and blaze your own path to greatness.

Dreams are for both young and old alike. Age doesn't matter. What matters is the youthfulness of heart and mind. Why do you think Disneyland is so successful? People want to feel young and dream about the unreal. But what is not real can become real. When this world was created, all that was here was land, water, and the natural resources. Look around you now; everything has been created, from paper to tires to buildings to movies to rocket ships. At one time, all these things were unimaginable. But at some point somebody had a dream, and they followed through with it, and persisted through many disappointments and failed attempts. That's why you have a car to drive, a cell phone, TV and computer. The individuals who invented and created everything you use, from a hairdryer to gasoline, had a dream and nothing would stop them from realizing it.

These innovators had three very important characteristics that helped them push through all the self-imposed barriers: Determination, Perseverance, and Endurance.

To push the boundaries of invention and do the impossible, many of these people had to ignore the negative feedback from friends, family, and critics. And now, despite legions of nay-sayers throughout history, we have used the Earth's resources to become a society filled with miracles. Albert Einstein once said that "there are only two ways to live your life. One is as though nothing is a miracle and the other is as though everything is a miracle."

We have the rest of our lives from this moment on to make our dreams happen. Live life from the seat of your imagination, for in the very center of imagination is found the idea of what you most want to be. I can't guarantee how long your life will be, so go for it while you still can. And who knows, maybe one small change in the way you live your life will serve to extend your life. Do not believe what you see, see what you believe.

THIS IS YOUR LIFE...
HAVE THE WILL TO PERSEVERE!

There is a four letter word that is woven into the fabric of my soul, and that word is WILL. I have always had the WILL to persevere, the WILL to believe in myself, the WILL to take action and the WILL to never give up. This word has given me the unyielding strength to conquer all the negative situations I've encountered. WILL has allowed me to make something positive out of my life. I came up with an acronym for W.I.L.L., about never giving up. There is always a way! You can do whatever you want to, but you must first have the WILL to follow things all the way through to success.

W-Whatever
I- Is
L- Lacking,
L- Learn!

There are those people who say, "I would have done something with my life if I had more time." Then there are those who say, "I could have been something if I had only applied myself." Or how about the ones who say, "I should have devoted more time to my family." Woulda, Coulda, Shoulda—but most of all, SHOULDA NEVER GIVEN UP!!!! Life is a test, and we have to face reality. Success comes from trying and trying again until finally you succeed. All it takes is a spark and for me that spark starts the flame of desire and the will to never give up!

When I was married at age 23, I didn't even have a job. I got laid off right before the wedding day. In fact, the night before our wedding, my wife's maid of honor called her up very concerned, and told her that she shouldn't marry me because I was immature and didn't have a job. When my wife told me about the phone call that night, I couldn't believe it. My wife sure had a lot of faith in me. Needless to say, it was awkward the next day when looking at the maid of honor. We stayed our distance, but I guess I can't blame her for what she did. She was just another person who didn't have faith in me.

My wife had complete faith in me. Why else would you marry an unemployed man? I am here to tell you that we were living off of love. Then my wife was laid off from her job a month after we were married. We were both unemployed, living off unemployment. We were living on noodles and frozen vegetables, with the occasional hotdog thrown in. The honeymoon marriage was short-lived, and now we were in the real world. It was a crazy time for us. We had lots of stress, arguments, and doubts about whether our marriage was even going to work. At one point we thought about calling it quits and going back home to our parents. But we had a meeting and decided we would be a team from that point on.

We had never lived with each other and barely even knew one another. We had only been dating for a few months before I proposed, and we were married just one year from the day we met. It was quite an eventful year. I just knew she was the one for me. When you know, you know. So right after we were married, we were completely broke and living off unemployment. We were having the hardest time getting along and wondering what we were going to do with ourselves. I finally found a job in sales and promised myself that I would never be broke again. With hard work I excelled at my new occupation, but I could never have done it without my wife's support and the WILL within me. I was determined to improve my life, and with that determination I succeed in providing a quality life for my wife and children. Before we had children, I was able to pay for my wife to complete her schooling at a California State University without taking out a student loan. I am proud of her determination to do the schooling and earn her degree.

There are two words that, when used together, really get under my skin. They are "I can't." Once you say those words, you are right! You have sold yourself out and will give up without a fight.

If you ever get into a situation where you want to give up, you will do much better for yourself by saying "I can do this," "I can make this happen," and, "I can win." Just the words "I can" produce more energy for your mind, and this will empower you. Life is hard, but only the tough-minded will get somewhere. Everything you want in life is within your reach. But you have to empower yourself to reach out and grab it. There is no comfort in being comfortable. Comfort comes from the strength earned from growing through discomfort. Comfort comes by gaining strength from adversity. Comfort is self-confidence. Comfort comes from knowing that you have the WILL to do whatever it takes.

"I've missed over 9,000 shots in my career. I've lost almost 300 games. 26 times I've been trusted to take the game-winning shot...and missed. I've failed over and over and over again in my life. And that is why I succeed." — Michael Jordan

Do not hesitate to exercise your WILL in order to take the actions necessary to shaping your life the way you want. Remember, this is *your* life, not your parents, teachers', church authorities', neighbors', friends' or boss's. Take control now so that when you are older, you won't let everyone walk all over you and make you subservient. You are equal to any other person, and nobody is better than you. We all have the same blood, we are of the same species, and that means nobody is greater than you. Not me, not the President of the United States. It's all a frame of mind.

I have been in the same room with people who are worth five-hundred million dollars, even billions. They are no different and no better than you or I. The only difference between them and the average person is that they took decisive action and "went for it." To make their dreams reality, they persevered through all the hard times until they got to where they are today. That's it! Their great success came from simply following things through to the end.

I designed this "reactionary mind map" that I hope will give you an idea of where you really are today. The big circle is the "Negative Nuclear Self." Surrounding this circle are examples of pressures that may be consuming your mind and overwhelming you. Each dot has another set of pressures, including too much time being taken from you and having doubts. The analysis can then be taken up another notch, and help point out another set of pressures.

By adding pressures upon pressures, and realizing how these pressures add up to create a massive burden, you can finally come to recognize the ways in which your mind continually acts like a broken record. Because you may be constantly trying to dig your way out of a ditch, you come to feel overwhelmed, like you're never accomplishing anything. You find yourself "ping-ponging" through life, lost in the maze of your mind. You go through the routines of life like a zombie, and are zombies happy? Not very.

The second, smaller circle is the one called "What Self Wants To Be." It is directly connected to and impacted by the negative aspects of ourselves. It is correlated with our mind, and our mind feeds us doubts about our ability to accomplish our personal goals. The negative pressures overwhelm our dreams, making them into a smaller priority than they should be. Doubts trickle into fear and fear leads to a failure to try anything. So much of our energy is spent dealing with the daily pressures that we may never take the time to do what we want to do, and that is accomplishing our dreams.

Use your WILL. We all have it somewhere buried in our hearts. To me WILL is the "Holy Grail" of building the life you've always wanted. It separates the achievers and those so-called "dreamers" who are unwilling to take action.

If you lack the WILL, you get the leftovers of what life has to offer. Go out into this world of limitless possibilities and make WILL your best friend!

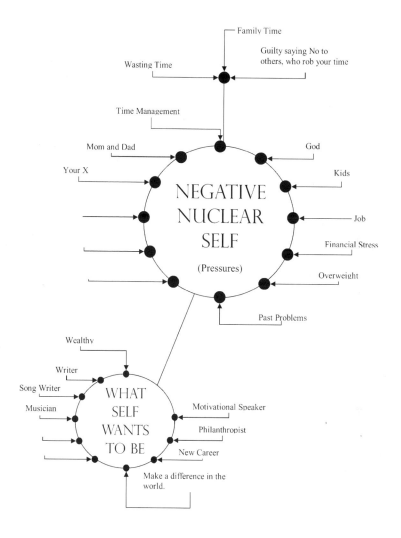

Family Time

Guilty saying No to others, who rob your time

Wasting Time

Time Management

Mom and Dad

God

Your X

Kids

NEGATIVE NUCLEAR SELF

Job

Financial Stress

(Pressures)

Overweight

Past Problems

Wealthy

Writer

Song Writer

Musician

WHAT SELF WANTS TO BE

Motivational Speaker

Philanthropist

New Career

Make a difference in the world.

PROCRASTINATE?
OR
PRO-ACTIVATE?

Here are a few things to consider when evaluating your current way of thinking and the life you're now living. Ask yourself these questions:

Am I self-sufficient?
Do I thrive or simply survive?
Does unbalance control me or do I control my balance?
Does time control me or do I control my time?
Does money control me or do I control my money?
Does food control me or do I control my food?
Does anger control me or do I control my anger?
Does passion control me or do I control my passion?
Do I try to find the humor in the things I do, or do I take things too seriously?
Do I let my body be a source of positive energy, or do I let it become a source of negativity?
Does sleep control me or do I control my sleep?
Do I live life to the fullest or do I live life with no fullness?

Don't let this life pass you by. This is the most important lesson to take from this chapter. Don't wait to live life and then lay there on your deathbed having regrets about not having done what you always wanted to do. Consider your future self, and ask if this person regrets having never taken the time, or not having had the guts to go for it. The cemetery will always be there. And a person doesn't have to be deceased to live in a graveyard. It just depends on whether you let yourself die before you've even died. You can take the safe and boring way, but this way guarantees that you will one day have regrets. Better to live the exciting life full of curiosity and opportunity. Either way you're going to end up in the cemetery, so why not live before you die?

Procrastinate or proactivate? This is one of the most important questions you will ever ask yourself. The way you answer this question will determine your destiny. It's that simple. Let me make it even simpler: you have two choices in life, TO DO, or TO NOT DO. The great thing about your life is that you alone have the power to decide. You decide your outcome through your actions. When you're debating between doing and not doing, it will be your actions that finally decide the matter.

So what holds people back from taking action? I believe it is fear of being uncomfortable and the fear of failure. I find it hard to believe that it's the fear of success, as I have often heard people say. We all want success and a better life, but some people aren't willing to make the effort required to achieve it. Settling for procrastination will make you a prisoner in your own world. This world is full of miracles, and there are endless possibilities. Depending on your outlook on life, you can either thrive in it or die in it. To thrive, you must have the passion for action. Love what you do. You should love your job, and if you don't, find a job that you do love. If you love it, you will excel at it. You will spend the majority of your day working. You might as well love what you do.

I believe procrastination is a major cause of sadness, depression, suicide, and financial despair. I have seen people imprisoned by depression. The depression takes over their whole mind and body, much like a disease. Sometimes it takes months to pull themselves out. Procrastination causes depression because when people procrastinate they allow things to pile up higher and higher, never taking the time to clear their mind of all the clutter. It becomes overwhelming, and soon it becomes too much work. Everything you've put off catches up to you at some point, and then you just burn out. Remember, procrastination is the ultimate thief of your time. I believe firmly in "not putting off until tomorrow what I can do today."

Chances are that if you procrastinate in one aspect of your life, such as business, you will also procrastinate in your personal life. You must live your life with urgency in order to accomplish your dreams. You should never forget about the present day and the moment you find yourself in, because it is all these tiny moments put together that determine the quality of your future. Every moment provides you with an opportunity to work toward a future that will profit you mentally, spiritually, and financially.

Remember the Parable of the Talents in the Bible? A master gives money to each of his servants before going travelling. Two of the servants invest his money – called talents - and earn interest, while the third buries the treasure and does nothing with it. When the master returns, he chastises the third servant for doing nothing with the gift he'd been given. I believe the word "talent" can be interpreted as meaning both money and an ability—literally, a "talent" we might have.

What I take from this parable is the lesson that it doesn't matter how much we have been given, what matters is what we do with what has been given. We are the masters over our mind and actions. We must do rather than wait. The servants who were rewarded had faith enough to make something more out of what they'd been given. It is interesting that the master says "you wicked and lazy slave" to the third servant. I know from experience that even after having worked my butt off, I sometimes got nowhere. This might translate into a loss of money and time. I wonder what would have happened if one of the servants had showed a loss, which might technically have been considered worse than the zero-sum gain of the servant who buried his talent. If I had to operate and show results within a specific time-frame, I would have had to claim a loss, and what would the master have done with me? Would he have penalized me for failing, or would he reward me for trying? I like to think that the master would have at least acknowledged a worthy effort, even if it did end up in failure.

I think this parable illustrates why people procrastinate. If they try, they might fail, and because they care about the image people have of them, the possibility of failure makes action too risky. I say screw the image and screw what other's think about you. Let actions speak for themselves. You should never give up on what you want. You never fail until you stop trying. Try, try and try. Anyone who ridicules or pokes fun at a person who is trying is the real "loser."

Something this parable didn't discuss is using one's talents to help others, being selfless instead of selfish. I wonder what the outcome would have been had one of the servants told his master that he gave his money away to the poor and needy, to bring them happiness and give them hope. I would consider it selfless and generous. Wouldn't this be noble too? Maybe more so than making money for the master. We shouldn't be selfish, always thinking "What can I get out it?" or, "What's in it for me?" Being generous and giving to people has helped me become a more tender and "real" man, not to mention richer in spirit. Moreover, there have been times in my life when I needed help. How can I accept help in good faith if I am unwilling to help others?

Do you know what the opposite of faith is? It is Fear. Faith and conviction in your actions is like food for your passion. It's hard to achieve positive results in any endeavor without faith and conviction. Doubt is what drives the final nails into our coffins. Remember, it's all in the way you look at things. Keep a positive attitude, stay focused, take action and anticipate the reaction. Test yourself. Look at your bank account and see how it makes you feel. Or get on the scale and see how much you weigh; are you happy with what it says? Now visualize the results you want. We all know these results are attainable because we see people everyday who have attained their desired results. It's not hard knowing what to do, because we all know what to do. The challenge is to do what we know we ought to. It's that simple. Focus on breaking it down to baby steps, because baby steps are motion, and motion makes things happen.

With every action you take there is a guaranteed reaction. Life renews everyday. Engage life, and it will engage you. Let us make the best of our lives!

"Time is more valuable than money. You can get more money, but you cannot get more time." **Jim Rohn**

FATHER TO SON, TIME WELL SPENT. FAMILY ALWAYS COMES FIRST!

Recently I had one of the most amazing life-changing experiences I've ever had. I want to share it with you because there was a part of me that was healed by it. It was a Saturday morning and my wife had just left to go shopping. My six year-old son was complaining about not having some toy that his friend had. He was starting to cry because Mom was not going to buy it for him while she was out shopping. He was getting very frustrated. I told him, "Son, don't worry about it, we are so fortunate to have what we have." He didn't appreciate that comment and when I asked him to pick up his coat, he stood there defiantly. I then said in a commanding, fatherly voice, "You had better have an attitude of gratitude." He ran to the couch, hid his head and started crying hysterically. I realized that yelling at him was not going to help him to stop throwing his fit.

I was standing in the kitchen and said, "Son, come here." He came, and I bent down to his eye level and said in a very loving voice, "It's all about having an attitude of gratitude. Did you know that when I was your age, I didn't even own a toothbrush or a bicycle. You are so fortunate to have those things. When I was your age, I didn't even a have a Mom or Dad who cared about me or loved me. I didn't have a real home or family to stay with." His amazed eyes just stared up at me, and for a moment I think he understood exactly what I was saying. I then said, "No matter what, before toys and friends, family comes first and I want you to know that I love you very much." I put my hand over my heart and said it again with tears starting to flow down my face. "I love you so much, son. When I was your age nobody ever told me that, and I want you to know I love you with all of my heart." My tears were flowing and my voice was trembling as I said those words. I wanted to make sure that he knew what a heart full of love felt like.

As I tearfully conveyed my love for the third time, I saw tears flowing from his eyes and he ran to me and gave me a hug. At that moment our hearts were pounding right next to each other. We were silent as we held each other, which made our hearts pounding seem all the louder. My mind wasn't anywhere but right there in that moment, feeling the love my son had for me. I held him in my arms, embracing him in pure love. I cried with him and told him how proud of him I was, that he was a great son and a great sibling to his brother and sister. I continued to tell him about the hard times I had had as a six year-old, a little boy who nobody wanted, and reminded him that he was so very lucky to have a Mom and Dad that love him with all of their souls. I picked him up and brought him to the couch and just held him in my arms like he was a brand new baby again. I held him for half an hour, just staring into his eyes and telling him how much I loved him and how lucky I was to have him as a son. I told him that he makes me appreciate life every day, and how he sets a great example for me. He was so in tune with my emotions, and it gave me a sense of closure and security. I gave him the love that was never given to me as a child his age. It amazed me that I was talking to him and loving him as if I were his age, wishing that someone had talked to me and held me like that. It was a very surreal experience.

I love all of my children with all my heart. They are so very precious. My 8 year old son is such a loving, detailed and thoughtful little man. My 6 year old son shows so much affection and is in tune with others feelings. My 4 year old daughter is just a little princess that is so girly and so thoughtful. She is such a little helper. My 3 month old son is just adorable and I look forward to seeing him develop into a great man. I love spending time with them, watching them grow and watching their minds develop and problem-solve. Do you remember the great memories of being a kid? We were all kids at one time. I invite you to close your eyes right now and think about some of the funniest memories of your childhood. Maybe it was building a fort, camping or jumping in the lake, fishing or dressing up like a princess. Think about the greatest times you had with your Mom, Dad and family. Maybe it was helping your Mom bake cookies, or piggy-back rides on your Dad, or wrestling with him or playing catch. Maybe it was just having your mother hold you, giving you that awesome motherly love. Maybe it was just going for a drive with Dad on an errand, and you were just happy hanging out with him.

It took me a while in fatherhood to realize that families should always come first. I was guilty of putting work, friends and hobbies before family. I have my wife to thank for helping me see the light. Children are unbelievable creations. I have seen friends whose work, church and friends come first. The cell phone is also a major distraction when you're having family time. I found that out. When we are with physically with our families, our minds should be completely with them too. Just like the old days. There never was a cell phone conversation to break up family time. I believe the family unit was a lot stronger back then than it is now. So many distractions are tearing down the family.

My foster family was probably one of the last families in America to get a microwave oven. My foster Mom felt that the microwave would destroy the family because it would no longer make eating dinner together a priority. In the past, if you came home late for dinner it would be cold, and you'd it make it a priority to get to dinner on time in order to have a warm meal. Thanks to the microwave you can now always reheat your food. We can learn a lot from our parents and grandparents.

HOW A LITTLE FOSTER KID GREW UP AND TOUCHED PEOPLE'S LIVES.

Who would have thought that a little foster kid who was given up on, diagnosed with retardation, learning disabilities, anger issues, and withdrawal from reality, could one day grow up to touch so many people? Don't tell me that you can't make a difference in someone's life. You can. I am proof! The following comments are just a fraction of the numerous emails and letters I have received. It is very humbling to have people write such nice things about me. They strengthen me and give me hope for a better tomorrow. They make me feel as if my life were on the right course. These comments are from a U.S. Marine Platoon stationed in Iraq. They heard my songs and wrote me some very wonderful comments about them. What is amazing is that most of this platoon never knew their Mom or Dad, and grew up in group homes or orphanages. They lived a life similar to mine. Take a read and share some tears with some of these great men and women.

DOC EAGLE: Derek, your CD, *Goodnight Soldier* is entirely first rate. It's a platoon favorite. I like your music because your themes are real. This might sound strange, but your song " I Wanna Be A Kid" reminds me so much of my wife because of the time I told her about my sordid life tale of being a foster child. My wife was my hero. She was a nurse and she was always there for every soldier who ever needed a caring, compassionate goddess in their hour of pain. She was the kindest soul that God ever sent down from Heaven. Her smile was like the rainbow after a Virginia thunderstorm, her voice was that of an angel. Our first date, she listened to the story of my harsh childhood. I knew I was in love with her, and was hooked and did ***not*** want to be hooked, I never had anyone reach out or love me when I was a child or a young adult—and

it felt messed up to be loved. That is how messed up I was at the time. So I thought I would tell her my most horrible secret and by doing that she would then run for the hills and I would not have to be in love with her. She did not run for the hills, she just took my hand gently and said, ***Doc, that is the past***. It was the best advice anyone ever gave to me. Her eyes were like two Hawaiian turquoise pools, I fell in them and no longer cared that I had fallen in love. I loved her so much I just would have died in her place on 9/11, had God asked me or given me the opportunity. That the Gentleman upstairs did not give me the opportunity to save my wife with my own life is a bone of contention I plan on discussing when I am called back to the eternal homeland. In the meantime, I try to do the right thing here on Earth until it's time to go home for dinner with my wife up in Heaven. I cannot count the times I have listened to your song "I Just Wanna Be A Kid." I want to tell you how it really helped me with my pain, both of childhood and with the loss of my wife. The child spirit is really in that song, it tells a good story, but it also gives hope. Keep on writing that awesome music.

KONG: Derek, my favorite song of yours is "Goodnight Soldier." I grew up a foster child like you. To me, my heroes are military Moms everywhere. If they only knew how much their sons and daughters in Iraq think of them, miss them, love them, and risk all to protect them and their future, I think they probably would feel so filled with pride that they would float away like birthday balloons up to the ceiling of the ballroom. I never knew my birth Mom or Dad, but I have been really fortunate while here, along with our entire platoon to be "adopted" by a beautiful lady stateside who allows our platoon to call her Mom. Semper Fi Moms everywhere! "Goodnight Soldier" always makes me think of the military Moms everywhere, worrying about us all. It's an awesome song.

CHERRY: Derek, I like your music because to me,

the kind of music you write is the kind that touches the soul deep. Your music makes me feel closer to God. God is my hero. He has somehow kept me alive and *keeping on keeping on* all these years, through a real harsh childhood in foster care and times prior to joining the Marines when I really did not think I would make it to adulthood. I think God sent the music to you, and it is beautiful you can share your talent with the world. God is always there for me, and has brought so many great people into my life; these jar buddies of mine, Sally, Danny, and just about the best friend I could ask for, War Dawg. He brought me to the US Marines, and they turned a sad young man into a Marine with goals, positive attitude, and honor, courage and commitment. Semper Fi, God! So when I listen to your music, that is what I am reminded of, all that is good in the world.

TEX: Dang-a-lang, Derek, your music is awesome. I grew up in foster care, and never had a Mom figure in my life. And then I came to Iraq as a Marine and met up with WAR DAWG. One day I was sitting around feeling sorry for myself. It was my birthday and no one really knew or gave a damn. My team leader, War Dawg came up and said, WASSUP TEX? I was so bummed I just shrugged. She said, CHEER UP DUDE, I HAVE THIS GREAT CD I AM GONG TO PLAY FOR YOU. War Dawg played your *Goodnight Soldier* CD, the track called "I JUST WANNA BE A KID." Dang that music just loosened the knot in my heart big time. The words of it really got me, and before I knew it I was telling War Dawg about my bad times as a kid. Forever your song will be the symbol of how I got that chip off my shoulder, and made me realize I had a platoon Mom, War Dawg. War Dawg is always going to be my best friend, and listening to that song of yours was the moment I knew it. War Dawg is my hero cause she is the only person who can out-shoot me on SAW, is not afraid to ride in the hot seat. She can make me laugh all the time, she puts up with my craziness. She is the best leader a jar could get. I would follow her into battle anywhere with nothing if need be. She likes dogs like I do, she never gets grossed out by anything we say, and she can pick good scorpions for our gladiator fights. Lets see what else, she always lets me have her peanut butter crackers out of her MRE's. Plus she is the only one that likes Derek Clark CDs as much as I do. Plus she will pick up a camel spider with her bare hands. Oh yeah, and she is really Momly. And she can run as fast as me. Lets see, what else, uh, oh yeah she can whup me in Kbar tosses and when everyone falls asleep from me talking she is the only one who will still talk to me and stay awake. Oh yeah, and we both like peppermints and peppermint Tic Tacs. Plus she is really good at video games. Not that we get to play them at this ratty FOB. Plus we both like the song "I JUST WANNA FLY," and both think it's the best song ever written. Thanks Derek!

SPIDER: Derek I like your music because it really describes what it is like to feel things deep and not be able to tell anyone. I had a pretty bad childhood. HOW BAD WAS IT SPIDER? Ha ha, it was so bad the orphanage attendants from hell made my DI [drill instructor] at boot camp look like Elvis's doting mama. So being used to abuse, I totally bonded with my DI. Actually he was a good guy. When I was about to give up on a lot of the things, like the weapons training [I had to qualify to be a Marine with corrected vision, these dang coke-bottle glasses would scare off even Bin Laden!—that's why the Marines really took me in, plus they can bounce EMP bombs off my lens to any target just by having Kong swivel my head around....] my DI facilitated me to realize I could do it, and I actually qualified as Expert, when I was worried I would get the boot out of boot. I have a lot of other heroes, but my DI is always going to be my first hero, he was like a Dad, a Big Brother, and a Best Friend all in one. And when I listen to your song "I Just Wanna Be a Kid,"—to me the emotion of that song describes to perfection the feeling I had when I broke through the past into the present positive state of being a US Marine. Thanks Derek, for writing that song. Good luck with your book as well. Semper Fi!

ORLEANS: Hi Derek. I think your music is awesome. My favorite song is "Goodnight Soldier," with fast second I JUST WANNA BE A KID. I asked our

Chaplain if I could play your song I JUST WANNA BE A KID when I got baptized over here. Our Chaplain is really funny, and never loses his cool. Picture this dude—this was my baptism: I JUST WANNA BE A KID is blasting out of the boom box held by one of my platoon buddies, turned up on like 90,000 decibels. Just as the Chaplain is baptizing me in the Gulf, a mortar landed in the water like about 25 feet from us and he just laughs and says *ORLEANS WE ARE BOTH GETTING BAPTISED TODAY...THAT SONG IS REALLY RIGHTEOUS YOU PICKED TO PLAY—WHAT IS IT?* right before the concussion in the water hit us and knocked us up on the beach like a couple of beach balls. But a miracle happened, the boom box playing your song did not get wet and there you were, still singing your heart out I JUST WANNA BE A KID! Our Chaplain is so cool. He knows just about everything about the Bible, and he is a good role model, he loves his wife and kids and his wife is his most important person and best friend in life. If I did not like being a Marine so much I would be a Chaplain. Well the Chaplain said your song is one of the most spiritual pieces of music he ever heard, cause it's from the heart. And damn real man, I feel the same way. Semper Fi, God Bless you and your family, and hang tough with your book, it will happen.

FORREST G: Hi Derek your music is the bomb. I

would just like to tell you I will never forget your song Goodnight Soldier. It's because I grew up in Foster Care and never had anyone really listen to me until I met War Dawg and she was my team leader. The first time I met her she was playing your song, Goodnight Soldier in the office. When I heard that song, I just had to sit down and chill, it was so beautiful a song. War Dawg taught me just about everything I did not know, and I know she knows lots more and will teach me lots more. War Dawg is my hero because no matter how many stupid questions any of us dumb jars ask her, she never makes us feel dumb and she is very patient all the time with us. She really listens when we talk to her, whether one on one or in the team meetings. War Dawg says we are all equals, and she calls us her Jedi Knights or Knights of the Round Table and everybody really feels like that—cause she always gives credit to what we have to say. She is my hero too because she is pure courage on two legs, she is funny, always making us laugh, and she is also "Momly" to us, she always knows what to say when times are hard, like when we lost Stryker. She is also not afraid of anything and she can shoot an M16 and SAW better than me or Tex. She is my best friend ever. And so when I listen to your song Goodnight Soldier, this is all the stuff I think about, and your song makes me feel all is worthwhile in the world, because your music is so beautiful.

FU MANCHU:. War Dawg told us you had a foster care childhood like all of us. Man when I heard that song I JUST WANNA BE A KID, especially the part where you sing from your kid-self perspective and man, the pain is just there. I totally related to that. I always missed having a Mom, even more than having a Dad. I would listen to the other lucky guys at my schools complaining about their mothers and really dude I just wanted to rip their hearts out. YOU **HAVE** A MOM, SHUT UP!!!—*is what I wanted to scream.* So your song always makes me think of the importance of a Mother. Because dang real if you don't have one you know how important a Mother is. I like your song, because it also reminds me of my team leader War Dawg. She is my hero because she is an excellent Mother. She raised four sons to be US Marines and even got a letter from her son's DI's saying in all their time in the Corps, they never saw a mother support her sons through boot camp like War Dawg did. This one DI wrote that the motivational letters War Dawg wrote to her son were so good he read them to their entire platoon. *When I was in boot camp I did not get one single letter, no moto ever, unless I did it myself.* Damn I bet you can relate to that feeling of being totally alone, because War Dawg told us you grew up similar. If I ever could know my birth Mom I would want her to be just like War Dawg. And she is the one that turned me on to your music. So to me your song will always be a huge thing and these are all the thoughts that go through my mind when I listen to it over and over again. Keep on writing such great music Derek, and God Bless.

FANGBOY: Yo Derek! Your music is the best. I just want to tell you that my favorite song is I JUST WANNA BE A KID. And why it is my favorite? It is my favorite because it always reminds me of my best friend Munch. Munch was my best friend when I was in the orphanage. That little dude had heart. He was born with a condition where he had a normal head but his body was the size of a toddler. He took a total rash from everybody who crossed his path every day of his life. But he was like a lion, man he could roar better than me, who was like gigantic. I met him when we were eight and we were best friends until he died when he was 16 from heart problems relating to his birth condition of being tiny. How we met was it was my first day at the home, and these bigger kids were ready to grind my face into the brick wall. Munch sped up in his electric wheelchair—knocked down the three bullies like dominos, rode over one of the bullies butt, and then yelled, LEAVE THE KID ALONE OR I WILL PERSONALLY RIP ALL YOU GUYS APART. I did not know whether to laugh or pee my pants, but the three bigger kids knew how to react, they booked to the border. And I don't mean the Taco Bell Border man. Munch looks at me and says, "If you are gonna survive in this dung hole you better learn to kick some butt." And we just kind of smiled at each other and were friends from that moment on. Munch's favorite band was Red Hot Chili Peppers, and his only interest was girls. Formidable dude, he would get more girls to dance with him anywhere, anytime than Brad Pitt probably could. And he could spin that wheelchair better than Michael Jackson could moonwalk. Every day I miss him. He had heart. To me, your song, I JUST WANNA BE A KID is like an anthem to Munch. Every time I listen to that song, I do cry, and think of him being free from his body that held him prisoner. He would love that song if he heard it too. What you write about, the pain, overcoming it, that was Munch every day of his life. What you do is awesome, hope you keep on doing it Derek. Thanks and Semper Fi.

BIG DADDY: Derek I am going to tell you my story so you will know how much your song I JUST WANT TO BE A KID means to me. My 'escape' happened when I was ten years old back in Mississippi. I had nine little brothers and sisters. My mama died when I was born, I never knew her. My daddy was a sharecropper, we was dirt poor, never even had shoes for school, except in the winter. He had a "second woman" as they called her. She was as mean as Godzilla and from her all my little sisters and brothers were born, she was even carrying my Dad's kid when my Mom died my Granny said. The platoon says my story sounds like the old school

DVD Grapes of Wrath, well it's not far off. They were funning me about my story until I pulled up my shirt and showed them all the scars from the whuppins I used to get. They thought the scars were always from schrap wounds I got here, but Doc Eagle set them straight, he said, "Dudes these were not schrap wounds," because no one would believe I got the scars as a kid. But anybody who took beatings as a child, they would know they are from my Dad's and Stepmama's whippins. I took 'em for the other kids as well. I didn't want the little ones to get that—thought I might as well get it all, save them the pain. So I stood in their place. Well one day I went to school, I passed out. I had not eaten any kind of full meal in about a week cause we kids was always short on food and I'd been giving my share to my little sister, Liza. I had just been given a fresh beating the night before, so blood had seeped through my school shirt. The teacher took me to see the nurse—and she freaked out big time and blew the whistle on my Dad and Stepmama. Well let me tell ya Derek, I did not want to go home that day. I knew the nurse was sending the sheriff and the county worker out to nail my Dad and Stepmama. I walked home like a zombie that day, knowing I was in for the worst beating of my life when my Dad got that visit from the social. I got home, the three littlest ones, Kara, Sue and Jimmie were all drenched in pee and poop, starving and screaming their heads off, all covered in baby snot. Liza, Cherie, Jamie, Tommy, Donnie and

Mikey were all starving as well—trying to do their school books, but so hungry they cold hardly sit up. No food any wheres in the shack, not even a crust of bread. Only good part was no Dad or Stepmama, so no more whippins. I was in no hurry to get the next beatin' when they found out that Nurse had a problem with my back and was sending the social around. I just sat down, and cried. I ain't ashamed to admit it. I bawled like the babies. I was so tired, so hungry and so scared. Just then there was a big banging knock on the door. I opened it and there on the step was the Sheriff. He saw the state of us and called the county worker to get over fast. By nightfall we were all in the county orphanage. My Daddy had a friend who worked in the school office, so she called and tipped off my Stepmama—and she went down to warn my Daddy at work what happened and that the Sheriff would be coming by. My Daddy and Stepmama were never found again—they just took off!

I don't think of my Daddy. But I think of all my brothers and sisters. Within fifteen months at the orphanage they had all been adopted out, the records sealed. They were good lookin' kids. I am glad for em all. I don't know where they all are today, haven't seen em since they all left the orpha age. But I pray God's looked out for em. I guess nobody wanted to adopt a boy with all the scars I had, so I was raised all my life at the orphanage, then went straight into the Marines at eighteen. Well I will never forget my little brothers and sisters. I like kids so much these Iraqi kids just tear my heart out—they are so cute—the good ones who haven't been taught to hate and kill like old men.

Someday I hope to have my own kids, a big family, that's if my future wife okays that—cause it will be her that does the greatest sacrifice to bring them in the world. What a mom does, a good mom, is huge—way huger than the part any Daddy puts in.

Long story comes to an end Derek—I was really protective of the little kids at the orphanage, they all called me Daddy! The minister and his wife that ran the orphanage started calling me Big Daddy to be funnin'. One of the little orphans I grew up with went into the Marines same time as me, and he called me Big Daddy and it became my jar name in my boot camp platoon.

When I hears that song of yours, I JUST WANNA BE A KID for the first time, it was like something burst inside me, like a balloon with too much water. I just cried for about five minutes. That song you wrote said it all for all the pent up emotions and hell I went through in the first part of my childhood. After I cried I felt 100% better and War Dawg just held me like a little boy till I got through the crying. That is the best song I have ever heard, and the best song I will ever hear, and thanks for writing it. When I listen to it now, I don't feel sad anymore, now it just reminds me of all the good things to come in the future, and how far I got down the road so far in a positive way.

TANK: My favorite song is by Derek Clark and its called Never Give Up. When War Dawg played that CD of Derek Clark's and I heard that song, my heart, something just came up from the depths of it, and I had to just cry at the end of it. That song is about my life, I said, when I heard it; because life was a real struggle for me. If the Marines had not taken me under their wing, I would definitely be dead by now. The Marines gave me a life; a career, self-respect—and it would have never happened if I had given up. Derek Clark's song is all about that. Anyone who had a struggle and overcame it would like that song.

ICEMAN: Hola Derek, thanks for doing what you do. My favorite song is I JUST WANNA BE A KID. Because that song is like my life story measured out in pain. I would be dead by now if Mike, a police officer who befriended me when I was fourteen had not come into my life. Up to that point I had no male role models worth anything. I was a total fool, and running with a bad crew, all older kids and dropouts, and if it had not been for Mike I probably would be in San Quentin waiting for Johnny Cash's second coming instead of being lucky enough to be a US

Marine and on this program. This crew I was with, they told me I was supposed to go in this 7/11 and rip off beer to stay in the gang. Well I go in to do it like an idiot, and Officer Mike pulls up in his squad car with his canine partner, and comes in for his Big Gulp and lard pill or whatever. I got the booze stuck in my skinny a— pants, oh yeah I was a real bad dude. I start booking past Officer Mike all cool, and he lets me get out of the store. Well crap I get out there, my homies all drove off! Officer Mike says, CAN I TALK TO YOU? He said, YOU LOOK LIKE A SMART GUY. YOU ARE TOO SMART TO BE DOING THIS STUFF. GIVE ME WHAT YOU TOOK I WILL STRAIGHTEN IT OUT THIS TIME. BUT DON'T YOU EVER BE OUT STEAL-ING AGAIN! I freaked out, handed him the 40 ounc-er of Budweiser, promised to not do it again. He did not skip a beat dude, he just takes out one of his cards, writes his home number on the back. He said, ask your folks if you can meet me for lunch at the McDonald's and then I will take you over to sign you up for PAL. We need some good football players...You play football son? I don't know what happened, but I just started crying. No one had ever really cared about me before. I told him I was an orphanage kid, the whole nasty history of my crappy life and abusive druggy parents who dumped me there. He did not even blink. He just says, THAT WAS THEN, THIS IS NOW...want a big Gulp? Wait here. Then he straightens it out with the 7/11 guy about the beer, returns it, comes out with a Big Gulp, Cheetos, a cheeseburger and a candy bar for me. He says, the 7/11 guy is cool as long as he knows you are sorry…oh yeah, by the way I got you a job in there, he needs help, it pays minimum wage and you can work M-F afternoons after school, so show up here tomorrow, got that, now want to ride with my partner and me and talk some more? He says. I get in the car, and his partner is like the coolest dog I ever met. Mike goes, This is Officer Lord Jim. That was the dog's name. So we rode around till his shift was over, hella cool, and then he took me home to meet his wife and kids, his wife Cindy was as nice as him and invited me to dinner and then called the orphanage to say I was in a police athletic meeting and Officer Mike would bring me back by curfew. After that I had a friend for life and that is why Officer Mike will always be the part of your song where you sing I JUST WANNA BE A KID. He and his wife even showed up at my boot grad, and I had no one else there so it was especially cool. So this is what goes through my head every time I hear your song I JUST WANNA BE A KID. You are an awesome person and talent Derek, War Dawg has told us a lot about you, and I saw your website—hope all goes well with your life. Man I hear you have a wife and kids too, that is big inspiration to me, I hope I am that lucky some day. God Bless.

TONTO: Hi Derek, nice to get a chance to tell you

how much the platoon and I are into your CD Goodnight Soldier. It's the one we play over here at least once a day. War Dawg told us you grew up in foster care like we all did, but that's not the reason we like your music so much, we like it cause its hella good music number one. I like the song Good Night Soldier; it reminds me of my Grandpops. Derek you ever seen or heard that Oliver Twist story dude? That was my orphanage all the way. All us Native American kids there would be shorn of our hair, our language, our culture, our families; the purpose was to integrate us into the dominant culture. Kids would get so depressed they would walk out into the below zero snow and just freeze to death trying to find their way home. Some of the abusive teachers would call these dead kids Injun Pops or Injunsicles. The government said we go, we went, did not matter if we had family or not. My Mom and Dad bit it when I was young, about two, in a rez wreck. I was in the back seat. I was just running around in the back of the truck bed, with about nine other drunken adults.

A rez wreck is too many Indians going too fast while drinking too much. When the pickup hit a semi, the whole thing just exploded, and I was thrown like thirty feet away, and woke up and wandered over to the accident scene. The cops could not believe it, my Grandpops said. But Grandpops always told me, *Tonto, you are alive for a reason. The Creator has good things for you to do.* So I had to go to a special orphanage for Native Americans, and it sucked big time. It was like Oliver Twist for real—rez style. It was in there I watched my favorite old-school television show which was the Lone Ranger and Tonto. Me being Native American, the Marines called me Tonto like joking around, and it just stuck. I don't really mind being called Tonto, actually I kind of like it, because if it were not for Tonto, Lone Ranger would not have his Mask, his MO, or the name of his horse—plus we NA's sometimes get tossed around a bit by people that don't dig NA's—and that dude Tonto, he always kept his cool, he was a classy dude, never cussing or acting the fool or becoming angry—so for me, he was a cool dude. Also NA culture is about helping your brother, and to the Wasichu, or Anglo culture, a guy is lesser when being a sidekick, but see, in NA culture, the guy that is the sidekick is the real spiritual one, really the higher one, cause he sacrifices himself for the good of the tribe or the cause. It is the same as Jesus, really...except NA's call God the Creator. So your song, Goodnight Soldier, Goodnight Friend, its really mellow and it reminds me of my Grandpops. He wanted to take care of me, but the system would not let him, they thought he was too old to take care of me. Well all these thoughts, is what your music makes me think of. Hope your book is read by everybody that needs to read it, and get help. It's awesome what you are doing Derek. As we Lakota Sioux say, Walk in Beauty Always My Brother.

STRYKER: Hi Derek, it's really great you want to hear what we think of your music, because the platoon thinks you are the best singer on the planet. War Dawg brought a copy of your CD here to the Sandbox and the first time I heard that song Goodnight Soldier, I just felt really proud to be an American. When we have open mike night, that song is always the number one request. It makes me really proud to be an American when I hear that song. Doc Eagle said we are not supposed to bore the heck out of you. But just tell you straight up what we think of your music. Well the day I had heard your song for the first time was the first day I got to Iraq. While your song was playing, Goodnight Soldier, I fell in love with an Army girl, Pam. I fell hard, she was going to be my future wife in my heart. But what I didn't know was that she was engaged to an Army guy in a Stryker Unit. This girl was loco, she had me meet her inside a Stryker vehicle—we didn't get past a couple of kisses and her Army guy shows up screaming her name in the bay—sticks his head in and catches her ready to plant the fourth lipstick kiss on my face. She had on this real pretty hot pink lipstick, it was Diabolique by Dior...and most of it was on my high and tight...Derek, after the Army guy and I had a rollover (fight) we went to have a beer together, sold from this guy that was selling illegal at a Sgt. Bilko base bar [Translation: Army Entrepreneur selling smuggled in beers]. I reached in my cammie pocket for some green and there was

Pam's lipstick. The Army guy and I couldn't believe it, either, but lipsticks have names! So that is how I know the official name of Pam's Lipstick. We hawed like hyenas and both about laughed to death. Turned out Pam was a big flirt and liked to make this Army guy jealous on a daily basis with the local jar imports. That's the whole sordid tale. Stryker Boy was then plastered on me by my platoon when they heard the tale of this. Now y'all know the whole sordid story of how I got my heart broken. So if you ever decide you need a good story about your music to quiet your fans when the electricity suddenly cuts out and they are about to riot, you can keep em subdued with this story about the dumb jar that lost his heart while your song Goodnight Soldier played in the background. Semper Fi, for serious Derek, your music is awesome. (Stryker wrote this to me before he was Killed in Action in Iraq, 2007)

IN CLOSING...

I would like to begin this final chapter with one of my favorite little stories about touching the lives of people who are in despair. I don't know who wrote it, but it perfectly describes having love and compassion for another.

STAR FISH

"One day as I was walking along the beach, I saw someone in the distance throwing something into the sea. As I came closer I could see hundreds of starfish that had washed up on the beach, and an old man who was carefully throwing them, one by one, back into the sea.

I asked him why he was doing this, and he told me that soon the hot sun would destroy the starfish that were on the beach, and he was throwing back as many as he could before this would happen.

I asked, "Why should you do this? Does it really matter?"

He picked up another starfish, then looked at me and said, "To this one it does."

-Anonymous

It's my hope that my story has touched your life, and if it has, that you share it with others in an effort to give them hope. If you know anybody suffering emotionally, mentally, or physically, and believe they could relate to my story, please share it with them. I believe that if you give hope, you are given hope in return. Everyone deserves a better life. Remember, the tiniest positive action you take is a step towards a better tomorrow. Action creates momentum, and with momentum your life will never be the same again. So if you think there is a problem in your life, you're right. Problems are self-made.

Don't think of life as having problems, think of it as having "situations." The word "situation" doesn't have the same negative connotations. Problems can seem insoluble, and may lead to inaction. But a situation seems open to remedy. Twists and turns make life more adventurous. This book has been about having the courage to never give up, no matter what life throws at you. If I Can Fly, You Can Fly! That is no joke, I have gone through hell and if I can do it, you surely can. So fly into this great open sky and achieve your dreams.

Live your life with passion. Be curious about what the world offers. Be creative in your solutions. Be honest with yourself. Live with excitement and a sense of adventure. Be determined to never let yourself down. Endure the hard times for they do end, and they are just a blip on the radar of life. Be happy with who you are and share your talents with others. Be giving to those who feel like they're losing the battle of life. Even if you are completely unaware of your influence, something as simple as your attention may help them find new sources of the energy that is necessary to prevail.

Be patient, life will happen no matter what. Before you know it, you will be an adult and then when you are an adult you wish you were a youth again. So take your time and enjoy your life as it is right now in the moment. Make choices that are true to you, for every action has a reaction. Don't react to life. Guide yourself with vigor and valor to the beautiful destiny you've dreamed of. Your Life is the pathway to your heart, and your heart is the pathway to your life. Dream big for beyond your dreams are the realities of tomorrow. Live ethically so that generations to come will know of your noble name. Above all, love. Let love in and love life, love yourself and love others. Love doesn't kill, love heals. Where there is love, there is peace. May you bear the promise of never giving up and always loving as if there will be no more tomorrows.

"When you come to the end of your rope, tie a knot and hang on."
-Franklin D. Roosevelt

I humbly thank you for reading my story and I hope to one day meet you at one of my seminars.

For more information on Derek's products and services, please visit my websites.

CONTACT ME

You can contact Derek Clark at

Derek@iwillnevergiveup.com

Visit Derek Clark's web site at
www.iwillnevergiveup.com
And
www.neverlimityourlife.com

Derek Clark is an inspiring speaker whose message conveys a "realistic" mix of hope, encouragement and determination by sharing his sad and triumphant experiences. On stage, his passion for life and music will touch and warm the audience's soul. He brings humor and the power of music to help others change their life. They will walk away with a new focus and the confidence to overcome any obstacles in their life.

To have Derek Clark be part of your next event, email
seminars@iwillnevergiveup.com

Email me, I would love to hear your story of overcoming adversity and how you Never Gave Up.

I WILL NEVER GIVE UP

BY DEREK W. CLARK

AWARD WINNING BOOK

The true and inspiring story about a foster kid who found
the light at the end of the tunnel.